# My First Resume

MW00889587

**Tip:** First, read the entire passage. After that, go back and fill in the blanks. You can skip the blanks you're unsure about and finish them later.

| qualifications | potential | improvements | grammatical | freshman |
| intimidating | leadership | habits | contribute | regular |

When you're a high school student, writing a résumé can be _____. The good news is that you probably have more work experience than you realize, even if this is your first résumé. Experiences such as childcare, yard work, and volunteerism all _____ to developing key work skills that companies seek. Simply because you have not held a position similar to the one you are seeking does not indicate you lack the requisite abilities to succeed.

Be sure to include any previous employment, especially if it was for pay. Other than that, you can consist of informal work such as pet sitting, cutting grass, snow shoveling, and any other tasks you've done for money. Although you may not have received a _____ income for your informal employment, your talents and reliability as an employee can still be shown via it.

Given that the majority of teenagers have not held many jobs, it is critical to draw on all elements of your life that prove you possess the attitude, willingness to work hard, competencies, and personality necessary for job success.

Please list any _____ positions you held (for example, a president of an organization or as team captain), as well as any honors or awards you have received. Include a list of your duties and accomplishments under each heading.

Employers are more concerned with your work _____ and attitude than anything else. Nobody expects you to be an expert in your field. When recounting an experience, you might use language to the effect that you have perfect or near-perfect attendance and are on time for school and other commitments.

Employers are looking for employees who have a history of positively impacting the company. Ask yourself whether there are any accomplishments that you can include from your time in school, your clubs, or your employment. Use verbs like "upgraded," "started," and "expanded" to describe what you've done if you want to illustrate what you've accomplished. To demonstrate to _____ employers that you are both bright and ambitious, include any demanding advanced academic assignments on your resume.

Keep it short: Keep it simple (But Include All Necessary Information). A single page is all you need. Contact information and previous work experience are both required in some way on every resume. On the other hand, you can exclude things like a career objective or summary.

Create a narrative. Match your talents and expertise to the job's requirements. For example, in the case of a cashier position, if you've never had a position with that precise title before, emphasize your customer service abilities, aptitude for mathematical calculations, work ethic, and ability to operate as part of a team. Examine the job description and make sure your _____ meet the requirements.

It is also appropriate to add information about your academic achievements, such as participation in organizations and the necessary curriculum you finished while producing a college _____ resume or a resume for a college application. Suppose you're applying for work as a front desk receptionist at a hotel. You could want to include the talents you gained while studying hospitality at a school.

Finally, be sure to double- or even triple-check your resume for typos and _____ errors. You may be tempted to send in your resume as soon as you finish it, but take a few minutes to review it.

As a last resort, ask for a second opinion on your resume from friends, family, or school teachers. Have them go it through to see if there's anything you missed or if you can make any _____.

# PRACTICE ONLY

## Employee Application

Employers use employment applications like this apart of their hiring process. It tells them about the potential employee.

### Applicant

Name:                                 Date:

Referral:                          Phone No.

Fax No.                          Email:

Address:

**Are You…**

| | | |
|---|---|---|
| A U.S. Citizen? | ☐ Yes | ☐ No |
| Over 18 years old? | ☐ Yes | ☐ No |
| Licensed to drive? | ☐ Yes | ☐ No |

### Employment

Position:                         Department:

Type:     ☐ Full-Time   ☐ Part-Time   ☐ Other (Seasonal/Temp):

Start Date:                     Starting Salary:

Current Employment:            May we contact?   ☐ Yes   ☐ No

### Education History

| Education | School | Location | Years | Graduated? | Degree(s) |
|---|---|---|---|---|---|
| High School | | | | | |
| College | | | | | |
| Graduate | | | | | |
| Other Training/Classes: | | | | | |
| Workshops/Certifications: | | | | | |

### Employment History

| Employer | Address | Position | Dates | Reason for Leaving |
|---|---|---|---|---|
| | | | | |
| | | | | |
| | | | | |

### References

| Reference | Relationship | Phone | Email | Address |
|---|---|---|---|---|
| | | | | |
| | | | | |
| | | | | |

Applicant Signature                              Date

The brag sheet, which is not to be confused with a student resume for college applications, is designed specifically for writing letters of recommendation. However, it is similar to a student resume in that it highlights your achievements, key experiences, leadership abilities, and employment throughout your secondary education. Brag sheets allow you to assist your educator(s) in writing letters of recommendation on your behalf. This form provides them with more information about who you are outside of school and your interests. You may not need a brag sheet right now, but it would be a good idea to practice filling out this form and sharing it with your parents, counselor, or teacher to request a letter of recommendation!

## BRAG SHEET
College Planning

## NAME:

### What is your anticipated college major?

### What colleges are you going to apply to?

**HS Activities: Please list your HS activities, including clubs, teams, etc., and write the grade in which you participated.**  **Grade**

|  | |
|--|--|
|  | |
|  | |
|  | |
|  | |
|  | |

**Community Service: Please list your volunteer work and/or church activities.**

**Awards: Please list any awards (academic and non-academic)**

**List 3 adjectives to describe yourself:**

**How excited are you about your future?**

**Rating**  ☆ ☆ ☆ ☆ ☆

# BRAG
# SHEET
## Life Skill

Students generally have little control over their recommendation letters other than who they choose to write them for and the relationships that necessitate them.

The purpose of a brag sheet is to benefit you while making the writing process as easy for your recommender as possible. As the title suggests, it's one of the best opportunities to brag about yourself. While the primary purpose of a brag sheet is to help guide a teacher recommendation letter, it can also be used for a variety of other purposes.

When you go to an interview for a college that you applied to, bring your brag sheet with you and hand it to the interviewer. It will provide them with a quick overview of your hobbies, academic performance, and future goals. Not only will it highlight the best aspects of you, but it may also lead to more in-depth conversations because they won't have to waste time asking about basic information that you were able to cover in your brag sheet.

Additionally, you can use it when applying to schools and writing essays. It can be difficult and overwhelming to come up with a topic for your essays.

Describe an event or activity that has had an impact on your life.

What are you most proud of and why.

List the positive influences in your life (family, friends, sports, teacher. etc.)

# Following High School, What Should You Do?

As a high school senior, you've accomplished a great deal.

This is the culmination of 12 years of hard work. So, what do we do next?

One big goal might be to find a career path.

There are multiple ways to get to your destination. It would help if you first determined your goals and then devised a strategy for achieving them.

Most jobs require a high school diploma or its equivalent. Other jobs require some education or training after you finish high school. If you want to work in certain professions, you'll likely need at least an associate's, bachelor's, master's, or higher degree.

There are a variety of post-secondary options available, including:

1. Four-year university or college
2. Community college with a two-year program
3. Certificate and trade programs
4. Gap year

**4-year College or University**

To earn a bachelor's degree in a specific field of study, students must attend a four-year college or university. Students earn a bachelor's degree to prepare for a career after college, or they may choose to enroll in a graduate program.

**Community College**

Community College offers an associate degree program. You can use this degree to start a career right away or transfer to a four-year university to finish your bachelor's degree. The cost of attending a community college is typically lower than that of a four-year institution.

Additionally, smaller class sizes, easier access to tutors, and connecting with instructors are all advantages of a community college. Students who struggled academically in high school may particularly benefit from these benefits.

**Trade School**

A vocational or technical school may also be referred to as a trade school. It teaches students how to perform certain tasks to land a specific job. You are given a diploma or certificate when you finish the course of study.

Dental hygienist, computer programmer, respiratory therapist, electrical engineer, plumber, mechanic, chef, and cosmetologist are examples of professions.

**Military**

Many high school students believe that joining the military after graduation is a viable option because it allows them to attend college for less money or even for free after completing their service term. The so-called G.I. Bill provides veterans with benefits for tuition, books, and housing, and it can provide students with peace of mind by allowing them to avoid incurring student loan debt while in school.

Many high school graduates who decide to enlist in the military have specific goals in mind, such as intelligence operations, diplomatic interpreting, and legal support for active duty and officer personnel. Many parents are worried that their child will be sent to a front-line area. Still, the military offers a wide range of career options within its branches, so many who enlist never see any combat action themselves.

## Job Corps

If you are between the ages of 16 and 24 and have a low income, you may be eligible for the Job Corps program. Students can earn both a high school diploma and college credit. Job Corps centers can be found across the United States. These programs offer free or low-cost housing, food, health care, financial assistance, and guidance in shifting into a new job.

Health care, construction, information technology, and homeland security are just a few of the many career options available. In addition to finding work or an apprenticeship, many Job Corps alums pursue further education or the military.

## Gap Year

Before starting college or a career, many young people take a gap year to explore their interests and earn money. This is when they don't go to school for a whole year. The majority of people who take a gap year use the time to either work full-time, volunteer, or travel.

Students who are determined to return to school after a gap year and complete their degree may suffer some academic setbacks. Still, they may also gain "street smarts" that will benefit them academically in the future. Short-term experiences like this can help students develop life skills that will be useful in college.

Taking a gap year doesn't always entail hopping on a plane and traveling the world. After high school, many students decide to take a year off to find a good job and save money for college. There are two advantages to this option: the ability to pay for college without relying on student loans, and the opportunity to gain work experience.

1. **Community College offers an _____ degree program.**
   a. bachelors
   b. associate

2. **Many young people take a ___ year to explore their interests and earn money.**
   a. gap
   b. half

3. **If you are between the ages of 16 and 24 and have a low income, you may be eligible for the _____ program.**
   a. Military Program
   b. Job Corps

4. **A vocational or technical school may also be referred to as a secondary school.**
   a. False - trade school
   b. True - secondary or post-school

5. **Community College offers an associate degree program.**
   a. True
   b. False

6. **To earn a bachelor's degree, students must attend a _____ college or university.**
   a. two-year
   b. four-year

# Test Your Mathematics Knowledge

1. To add fractions_____
   a. the denominators must be the same
   b. the denominators can be same or different
   c. the denominators must be different

2. To add decimals, the decimal points must be?
   a. column and carry the first digit(s)
   b. lined up in any order before you add the columns
   c. lined up vertically before you add the columns

3. When adding like terms_____
   a. the like terms must be same and they must be to the different power.
   b. the exponent must be different and they must be to the same power.
   c. the variable(s) must be the same and they must be to the same power.

4. The concept of math regrouping involves_____
   a. regrouping means that $5x + 2$ becomes $50 + 12$
   b. the numbers you are adding come out to five digit numbers and 0
   c. rearranging, or renaming, groups in place value

5. _____ indicates how many times a number, or algebraic expression, should be multiplied by itself.
   a. Denominators
   b. Division-quotient
   c. Exponent

6. _____ is the numerical value of a number without its plus or minus sign.
   a. Absolute value
   b. Average
   c. Supplementary

7. Any number that is less than zero is called_____
   a. Least common multiple
   b. Equation
   c. Negative number

8. $23 = 2 \times 2 \times 2 = 8$, 8 is the
   a. third power of 2
   b. first power of 2
   c. second power of 2

9. -7, 0, 3, and 7.12223 are
   a. all real numbers
   b. all like fractions
   c. all like terms

10. How do you calculate $2 + 3 \times 7$?
    a. $2 + 3 \times 7 = 2 + 21 = 23$
    b. $2 + 7 \times 7 = 2 + 21 = 35$
    c. $2 + 7 \times 3 = 2 + 21 = 23$

11. How do you calculate (2 + 3) x (7 - 3)?
    a. (2 + 2) x (7 - 3) = 5 x 4 = 32
    b. (2 + 3) x (7 - 3) = 5 x 4 = 20
    c. (2 + 7) x (2 - 3) = 5 x 4 = 14

12. The Commutative Law of Addition says_____
    a. positive - positive = (add) positive
    b. that it doesn't matter what order you add up numbers, you will always get the same answer
    c. parts of a calculation outside brackets always come first

13. The Zero Properties Law of multiplication says_____
    a. that any number multiplied by 0 equals 0
    b. mathematical operation where four or more numbers are combined to make a sum
    c. Negative - Positive = Subtract

14. Multiplication is when you_____
    a. numbers that are added together in multiplication problems
    b. take one number and add it together a number of times
    c. factor that is shared by two or more numbers

15. When multiplying by 0, the answer is always_____
    a. 0
    b. -0
    c. 1

16. When multiplying by 1, the answer is always the _____
    a. same as the number multiplied by 0
    b. same as the number multiplied by -1
    c. same as the number multiplied by 1

17. You can multiply numbers in_____
    a. any order and multiply by 2 and the answer will be the same
    b. any order you want and the answer will be the same
    c. any order from greater to less than and the answer will be the same

18. Division is____
    a. set of numbers that are multiplied together to get an answer
    b. breaking a number up into an equal number of parts
    c. division is scaling one number by another

19. If you take 20 things and put them into four equal sized groups
    a. there will be 6 things in each group
    b. there will be 5 things in each group
    c. there will be 10 things in each group

20. The dividend is_____
    a. the number you are multiplied by
    b. the number you are dividing up
    c. the number you are grouping together

21. The divisor is _____
    a. are all multiples of 3
    b. the number you are dividing by
    c. common factor of two numbers

22. The quotient is _____
    a. the answer
    b. answer to a multiplication operation
    c. any number in the problem

23. When dividing something by 1_____
    a. the answer is the original number
    b. the answer produces a given number when multiplied by itself
    c. the answer is the quotient

24. Dividing by 0_____
    a. the answer will always be more than 0
    b. You will always get 1
    c. You cannot divide a number by 0

25. If the answer to a division problem is not a whole number, the number(s) leftover_____
    a. are called the Order Property
    b. are called the denominators
    c. are called the remainder

26. You can figure out the 'mean' by_____
    a. multiply by the sum of two or more numbers
    b. adding up all the numbers in the data and then dividing by the number of numbers
    c. changing the grouping of numbers that are added together

27. The 'median' is the_____
    a. last number of the data set
    b. middle number of the data set
    c. first number of the data set

28. The 'mode' is the number_____
    a. that appears equal times
    b. that appears the least
    c. that appears the most

29. Range is the_____
    a. difference between the less than equal to number and the highest number.
    b. difference between the highest number and the highest number.
    c. difference between the lowest number and the highest number

30. Please Excuse My Dear Aunt Sally: What it means in the Order of Operations is____
    a. Parentheses, Exponents, Multiplication and Division, and Addition and Subtraction
    b. Parentheses, Equal, Multiplication and Decimal, and Addition and Subtraction
    c. Parentheses, Ellipse, Multiplication and Data, and Addition and Subtraction

31. A ratio is_____
    a. a way to show a relationship or compare two numbers of the same kind
    b. short way of saying that you want to multiply something by itself
    c. he sum of the relationship a times x, a times y, and a times z

32. Variables are things_____
    a. that can change or have different values
    b. when something has an exponent
    c. the simplest form using fractions

33. Always perform the same operation to_____of the equation.
    a. when the sum is less than the operation
    b. both sides
    c. one side only

34. The slope intercept form uses the following equation:
    a. $y = mx + b$
    b. $y = x + ab$
    c. $x = mx + c$

**35.** The point-slope form uses the following equation:

    a. y - y1 = m(y - x2)

    b. y - y1 = m(x - x1)

    c. x - y2 = m(x - x1)

**36.** Numbers in an algebraic expression that are not variables are called____

    a. Square

    b. Coefficient

    c. Proportional

**37.** A coordinate system is _____

    a. a type of cubed square

    b. a coordinate reduced to another proportion plane

    c. a two-dimensional number line

**38.** Horizontal axis is called_____

    a. h-axis

    b. x-axis

    c. y-axis

**39.** Vertical axis is called____

    a. v-axis

    b. y-axis

    c. x-axis

**40.** Equations and inequalities are both mathematical sentences____

    a. has y and x variables as points on a graph

    b. reduced ratios to their simplest form using fractions

    c. formed by relating two expressions to each other

# Geography: Time Zones

First, go over the entire message. Then go back and fill in the blanks. You can skip the blanks you're unsure about and come back to them later.

| | | | | |
|---|---|---|---|---|
| different | outside | message | shines | classmate |
| exist | clocks | time | ball | day |

Have you ever tried to call or send a _____ to someone who was on the other side of the country or the world? It can be tough to reach a faraway location from you because the time of _____ may be different from your own. The purpose of time zones and why we have them will be discussed in this session.

Kim, Mike's _____ who recently relocated across the country, is texting him. After a short time, Kim sends Mike a text message saying that it is time for her to go to sleep for the night. The sun is beaming brightly _____, and Mike is confused about why Kim would choose this time of day to go to sleep. 'Can you tell me what _____ it is, please?' Mike asked. 'It's 9:00 p.m. now!' Kim replies.

What exactly is going on here? Was Mike able to travel back in time in some way?

What is happening to Mike and Kim is nothing more than a natural occurrence that occurs on our planet daily. Since Kim relocated across the country, she is now in a _____ time zone than she was previously.

A time zone is a geographical location on the planet with a fixed time that all citizens can observe by setting their _____ to that time. As you go from east to west (or west to east) on the globe's surface, you will encounter different time zones. The greater the distance traveled, the greater the number of time zones crossed.

Time zones are not something that arises in nature by chance. Humans created the concept of time zones and determined which regions of the world are located in which time zones.

Because of time zones, everyone experiences the same pattern of dawn in the early morning and sunset in the late afternoon. We require time zones because the earth is shaped like a _____ and therefore requires them. As the sun beams down on the planet, not every location receives the same amount of sunshine. The sun _____ on one side of the earth and brightens it during the day, while the other side is dark during the night (nighttime). If time zones didn't _____, many people worldwide would experience quite strange sunshine patterns during the day if there were no time zones.

One key skill that everyone should be able to perform is determining whether a location on earth is in a later or earlier time zone than they are. The general guideline is as follows:

If your friend lives in a location that is west of you, they are in a different time zone than you. If they live in a time zone later than yours, they are located east of you.

West is considered to be earlier, whereas the east is considered later.

The following are the primary time zones in the United States:
Eastern (New York, Georgia, Ohio, and other east coast states)
Central (Alabama, Iowa, Minnesota, and more)
Mountain (Arizona, Montana, Utah, and more)
Pacific (California, Nevada, and other west coast states)

# Science: Albert Einstein

Score: _____

Date: _____

First, read the entire passage. After that, go back and fill in the blanks. You can skip the blanks you're unsure about and finish them later.

| | | | | |
|---|---|---|---|---|
| mathematics . | boat | Nobel | overnight | top |
| experiment | paper | books | Germany | failed |
| pocket | marriage | missed | socks | door |

Albert Einstein was born in _____ on March 14, 1879. Because he was Jewish, he fled to the United States to avoid Hitler and the Second World War.

When his grandmother first saw him, she said he was stupid! Little did she know!

He apparently didn't speak until he was four years old, and even then, he would repeat words and sentences until he was seven.

His father gave him a simple _____ compass when he was about five years old, and it quickly became his favorite toy!

He became obsessed with magnetism, which is basically all about magnets and how they work, from that day forward.

Young Einstein didn't like the way his grammar school taught him. He also wasn't particularly fond of authority. As a result, he was expelled from school quite a few times.

He developed an interest in _____ and science at the age of seven.

When Einstein was about ten years old, a much older friend gave him a large stack of science, mathematics, and philosophy _____.

He'd published his first scientific _____ by the age of sixteen. That is absolutely incredible!

Numerous reports have shown that Einstein _____ math in school, but his family has stated that this is not the case. They claimed he was always at the _____ of his class in math and could solve some challenging problems. He was obsessed with geometry and algebra, and no one taught him anything – he taught himself! He was also constantly attempting to prove various mathematical theories on his own.

Yes, he was brilliant.

Although he was not a top student in every subject in school, he certainly made up for it when he and his family moved to Switzerland when he was older.

He began teaching math and physics in 1900.

Einstein was a little disorganized. So, if you're feeling the same way, don't despair; there is still hope!

As an adult, he frequently _____ appointments, and because his mind was all over the place, his lectures were a little difficult to understand.

He didn't wear _____ and had uncombed hair! Even at posh dinners, he'd arrive unkempt, with crumpled clothes and, of course, no socks!

Despite the fact that he was all over the place, a little shabby, and a little difficult to understand, he rocked the world with his Theory of Relativity in 1915. An _____ in 1919 proved the theory correct. He became famous almost _____, and he suddenly received invitations to travel worldwide, as well as honors from all over the world!

In 1921, he was awarded the _____ Prize for Physics. He'd come a long way from the boy who was told he'd never amount to anything!

Today, his other discoveries enabled us to have things like garage _____ openers, televisions, and DVD players. Time magazine named him "Person of the Century" in 1999.

One of his favorite activities was to take a _____ out on a lake and take his notebook with him to think and write everything down. Perhaps this is what inspired him to create his inventions!

Einstein's first _____ produced two sons. His daughter, Lierserl, is believed to have died when she was young. He married twice, and she died before him.

On April 18, 1955, the great scientist died in America.

# Government History: How Laws Are Made

Congress is the federal government's legislative branch, and it is in charge of making laws for the entire country. Congress is divided into two legislative chambers: the United States Senate and the United States House of Representatives. Anyone elected to either body has the authority to propose new legislation. A bill is a new law proposal.

People living in the United States and its territories are subject to federal laws.

Bills are created and passed by Congress. The president may then sign the bills into law. Federal courts may examine the laws to see if they are in accordance with the Constitution. If a court finds a law to be unconstitutional, it has the authority to overturn it.

The United States government has enacted several laws to help maintain order and protect the country's people. Each new law must be approved by both houses of Congress as well as the President. Before it becomes a new law in the nation, each law must go through a specific process.

The majority of laws in the United States begin as bills. An idea is the starting point for a bill. That thought could come from anyone, including you! The idea must then be written down and explained as the next step. A bill is the name given to the first draft of an idea. The bill must then be sponsored by a member of Congress. The sponsor is someone who strongly supports the bill and wishes to see it become law. A Senator or a member of the House of Representatives can be the sponsor.

The bill is then introduced in either the House or the Senate by the bill's sponsor. Once submitted, the bill is given a number and is officially recorded as a bill.

The bill is assigned to a committee after it is introduced. Committees are smaller groups of congress members who are experts in specific areas. For example, if the bill concerns classroom size in public schools, it would be referred to the Committee on Education. The committee goes over the bill's specifics. They bring in experts from outside Congress to testify and debate the bill's pros and cons.

The committee may decide to make changes to the bill before it is passed. If the committee finally agrees to pass the bill, it will be sent to the House or Senate's main chamber for approval.

If the bill was introduced in the House, it would first be considered by the House. The bill will be discussed and debated by the representatives. House members will then vote on the bill. If the bill is passed, it will be sent to the Senate for consideration.

The Senate will then follow the same procedure. It will discuss and debate the bill before voting. If the Senate approves the bill, it will be sent to the President.

The President's signature is the final step in a bill becoming law. When the President signs the bill, it becomes law.

The President has the option of refusing to sign the bill. This is known as a veto. The Senate and House can choose to override the President's veto by voting again. The bill must now be approved by a two-thirds majority in both the Senate and the House to override the veto.

A bill must be signed into law by the President within 10-days. If he does not sign it within 10-days, one of two things may occur:

1) It will become law if Congress is in session.

2) It will be considered vetoed if Congress is not in session (this is called a pocket veto).

1. **If the Senate approves the bill, it will be sent to the _____.**
   a. President
   b. House Representee

2. **The _____ may decide to make changes to the bill before it is passed.**
   a. governor
   b. committee

3. **The bill must then be _____ by a member of Congress.**
   a. signed
   b. sponsored

4. **The President has the option of refusing to sign the bill. This is known as a ___.**
   a. voted
   b. veto

5. **The Senate and House can choose to override the President's veto by _____ again.**
   a. creating a new bill
   b. voting

6. **The bill is assigned to a committee after it is _____.**
   a. introduced
   b. vetoed

7. **Bills are created and passed by _____.**
   a. The House
   b. Congress

8. **A bill must be signed into law by the President within ___-days.**
   a. 10
   b. 5

9. **The President's _____ is the final step in a bill becoming law.**
   a. signature
   b. saying yes

10. **If the committee agrees to pass the bill, it will be sent to the House or Senate's main ___ for approval.**
    a. chamber
    b. state

Extra Credit: What are some of the weirdest laws in the world? List at least 5.

_____

_____

_____

_____

_____

_____

_____

_____

_____

_____

_____

_____

_____

_____

_____

_____

_____

# History: United States Armed Forces

The President of the United States is the Commander in Chief of the United States Armed Forces.

The United States, like many other countries, maintains a military to safeguard its borders and interests. The military has played an essential role in the formation and history of the United States since the Revolutionary War.

The **United States Department of Defense** (DoD) is in charge of controlling each branch of the military, except the United States Coast Guard, which is under the control of the Department of Homeland Security.

The Department of Defense is the world's largest 'company,' employing over 2 million civilians and military personnel.

The United States military is divided into six branches: the Air Force, Army, Coast Guard, Marine Corps, Navy, and Space Force.

The mission of the **United States Air Force** is to defend the country from outside forces. They also provide air support to other branches of the military, such as the Army and Navy.

The **United States Army** is responsible for defending against aggression that threatens the peace and security of the United States.

There are **Army National Guard** units in all 50 states, which their respective governments govern. The Constitution requires only one branch of the military. Members of the National Guard volunteer some of their time to keep the peace. They are not full-time soldiers, but they respond when called upon, for example, to quell violence when the police need assistance.

The primary concern of **the United States Coast Guard** is to protect domestic waterways (lakes, rivers, ports, etc.). The Coast Guard is managed by the United States Department of Homeland Security.

The **Marines** are a quick-response force. They are prepared to fight on both land and sea. The Marine Corps is a branch of the United States Navy. The Marine Corps conducts operations onboard warfare ships all over the world.

The **United States Navy** conducts its missions at sea to secure and protect the world's oceans. Their mission is to ensure safe sea travel and trade.

The **United States Space Force** is the newest branch of the military, established in December 2019. The world's first and currently only independent space force. It is in charge of operating and defending military satellites and ground stations that provide communications, navigation, and Earth observation, such as missile launch detection.

1. **The United States military is divided into ___ branches.**
   a. six
   b. five

2. **_____ is managed by the United States Department of Homeland Security.**
   a. The National Guard
   b. The Coast Guard

3. **The _____ of the United States is the Commander in Chief of the United States Armed Forces.**
   a. Governor
   b. President

4. **The United States maintains a military to safeguard its _____ and interests.**
   a. borders
   b. cities

5. **DoD is in charge of controlling each _____ of the military.**
   a. branch
   b. army

6. **The Marines are prepared to fight on both land and ____.**
   a. battlefield
   b. sea

7. **The United States Space Force is in charge of operating and defending military ____ and ground stations.**
   a. soldiers
   b. satellites

8. **The mission of the _____ is to defend the country from outside forces.**
   a. United States DoD Forces
   b. United States Air Force

9. There are _____ units in all 50 states.
   a. Army National Guard
   b. Armed Nations Guard

10. The United States Navy conducts its missions at sea to secure and protect the world's _____.
   a. oceans
   b. borders

11. The primary concern of the United States Coast Guard is to protect_____.
   a. domestic waterways
   b. domesticated cities

12. The United States military is: the Amy Force, Army, Coast Guard, Mario Corps, Old Navy, and Space Force.
   a. True
   b. False

Extra Credit: Has America ever been invaded?

_____

_____

_____

_____

_____

_____

_____

_____

_____

_____

_____

_____

_____

_____

_____

_____

# Grammar: Adjectives Matching

Adjectives are words that describe people, places, and things, or nouns. Adjectives are words that describe sounds, shapes, sizes, times, numbers/quantity, textures/touch, and weather. You can remember this by saying to yourself, "an adjective adds something."

If you need to describe a friend or an adult, you can use words that describe their appearance, size, or age. When possible, try to use positive words that describe a person.

| # | | Word | | Clue | Letter |
|---|---|------|---|------|--------|
| 1 | | disappointed | | nothing frightens him/her | A |
| 2 | | anxious | | everything is in order around him | B |
| 3 | | delighted | | very pleased | C |
| 4 | | terrified | | always arrives in time | D |
| 5 | | ashamed | | loves being with people | E |
| 6 | | envious | | very surprised and upset | F |
| 7 | | proud | | very frightened | G |
| 8 | | shocked | | wanting something another person has | H |
| 9 | | brave | | feeling bad because you did sg wrong | I |
| 10 | | hard-working | | uprightness and fairness | J |
| 11 | | organized | | worried | K |
| 12 | | punctual | | has 2 or more jobs | L |
| 13 | | honest | | always supports his friends | M |
| 14 | | outgoing | | feeling pleased and satisfied | N |
| 15 | | loyal | | sad because something is worse than expected | O |
| 16 | | reliable | | one can always count on him | P |

# History: The Thirteen Colonies

In 1776, thirteen British colonies merged to form the United States. Many of these colonies had existed for well over a century, including Virginia's first colony, founded in 1607.

A colony is a region of land that is politically controlled by another country. As was the case with England and the American colonies, the controlling country is usually physically distant from the colony. Colonies are typically founded and settled by people from the home country, but settlers from other countries may also be present. This was especially true of the American colonies, which people from all over Europe populated.

Here is a list of the thirteen colonies, along with the year they were established () and a description of how they were established.

**Virginia:** John Smith and the London Company set out for Virginia in 1607.

**New York:** The Dutch founded New York in 1626. In 1664, it became a British colony.

**New Hampshire:** John Mason was the first landholder in New Hampshire (1623). Eventually, John Wheelwright.

**Massachusetts Bay:** Puritans seeking religious freedom in Massachusetts Bay (1630).

**Maryland** (1633) - George and Cecil Calvert established it as a safe haven for Catholics.

**Connecticut** (1636) - Thomas Hooker, who had been ordered to leave Massachusetts.

**Rhode Island**: Roger Williams founded Rhode Island (1636) to provide a place of religious freedom for all.

**Delaware**: Peter Minuit and the New Sweden Company founded Delaware in 1638. In 1664, the British took over.

**North Carolina** (1663) - Originally a part of the Carolina Province. Separated from South Carolina in 1712.

**South Carolina** (1663) - Originally a part of the Carolina Province. In 1712, South Carolina seceded from North Carolina.

**New Jersey** (1664) - Initially settled by the Dutch, the English took control in 1664.

**Pennsylvania** (1681) William Penn and the Quakers.

**Georgia** (1732) - James Oglethorpe as a debtor's settlement.

Queen Elizabeth desired to establish colonies in the Americas to expand the British Empire and compete with the Spanish. The English hoped to find riches, create new jobs, and develop trade ports along the Americas' coasts.

Each colony, on the other hand, has its distinct history of how it was founded. Many of the colonies were established by religious leaders or groups seeking religious liberty. Pennsylvania, Massachusetts, Maryland, Rhode Island, and Connecticut were among these colonies. Other colonies were established solely to create new trade opportunities and profits for investors.

The colonies are frequently divided into New England Colonies, Middle Colonies, and Southern Colonies.

**New England Colonies:** Connecticut, Massachusetts Bay, New Hampshire, Rhode Island

**Middle Colonies:** Delaware, New Jersey, New York, Pennsylvania

**Southern Colonies:** Georgia, Maryland, North Carolina, South Carolina, Virginia

1. **The Dutch founded _____ in 1626.**
   a. New Jersey
   b. New York

2. **13 British colonies merged to form the_____.**
   a. United Kingdom
   b. United States

3. **Roger Williams founded _____.**
   a. Maryland
   b. Rhode Island

4. **A colony is a region of _____ that is politically controlled by another country.**
   a. land
   b. township

5. **Middle Colonies:**
   a. Delaware, New Jersey, New York, Pennsylvania
   b. Georgia, Maryland, North Carolina, South Carolina, Texas

6. **Colonies are typically founded and settled by people from the ____ country.**
   a. home
   b. outside

7. **Southern Colonies:**
   a. Maine, New Jersey, New York, Pennsylvania
   b. Georgia, Maryland, North Carolina, South Carolina, Virginia

8. **Many of the colonies were established by _____leaders or groups seeking religious liberty.**
   a. political
   b. religious

9. **New England Colonies:**
   a. Connecticut, Massachusetts Bay, New Hampshire, Rhode Island
   b. Ohio, Tennessee, New York, Pennsylvania

10. **George and Cecil Calvert established _____ as a safe haven for Catholics.**
    a. Maine
    b. Maryland

11. **The colonies are frequently divided into_____.**
    a. New England Colonies, Middle Colonies, and Southern Colonies
    b. United England Colonies, Midland Colonies, and Southern Colonies.

# Confusing Vocab Words

Because English is filled with words that look or sound alike (or both), but mean very different things, it's easy to become confused and use the incorrect word at the wrong time. However, if you are aware of the various meanings of these words, you will not fall into the same traps.

Fill in the blank with the best answer.

1. He _____ [ accepts / accept / excepts ] defeat well.

2. Please take all the books off the table _____ [ exception / accept / except ] for the thick one.

3. Lack of sleep _____ [ affects / affect / effect ] the quality of your work.

4. The _____ [ effects / affect / effect ] of the light made the room bright.

5. I have a _____ [ alot / lot / lots ] of friends.

6. The magician preformed a great _____. [ illusion / allusion / trick ]

7. Dinner was all _____ [ already / good / ready ] when the guests arrived.

8. The turkey was _____ [ al ready / already / all ready ] cooked when the guests arrived.

9. _____, [ All together / Altogether / altogether ] I thought it was a great idea!

10. We were all _____ [ altogether / group / together ] at the family reunion.

11. The fence kept the dogs _____. [ apart / a part / parted ]

12. A _____ [ section / part / Apart ] of the plan is to wake up at dawn.

13. The plane's _____ [ assent / descent / ascent ] made my ears pop.

14. You could see his _____ [ breath / breathing / breathe ] in the cold air.

15. If you don't _____, [ breath / breathe / breathing ] then you are dead.

16. The _____ [ capital / capitol / city ] of Hawaii is Honolulu.

17. That is the _____ [ capital / capitol / captain ] building.

18. I _____ [ sighted / sited / cited ] 10 quotes from the speech.

19. You can not build on that _____. [ cite / sight / site ]

20. The _____ [ cite / site / sight ] of land is refreshing.

21. I _____ [ complimented / complemented / discouraged ] my wife on her cooking.

22. We all have a _____ [ conscience / mind / conscious ] of right and wrong.

23. The boxer is still _____. [ conscience / conscious / knocked out ]

24. I went to the city _____ [ municipal / counsel / council ] meeting.

25. My accountant _____ [ directed / counciled / counseled ] me on spending habits.

26. The teacher _____ [ brought out / illicit / elicited ] the correct response.

27. The criminal was arrested for _____ [ elicit / illicit / illegal ] activities.

28. The baby will cry as soon as _____ [ its' / it's / its ] mother leaves.

29. _____ [ It's / It is / Its ] a beautiful day

30. I have a headache, so I'm going to _____ [ lay / lain / lie ] down.

31. You should never tell a _____. [ lay / lie / lye ]

32. If you _____ [ lose / find / loose ] your phone, I will not buy a new one!

33. My pants feel _____, [ loose / tight / lose ] I need a belt.

34. I _____ [ kindly / kind / a bit ] of like spicy food.

35. He is a very _____ [ kind of / mean / kind ] teacher.

# Math: Arithmetic Refresher

Score: _____

Date: _____

Select the best answer for each question.

1.  Use division to calculate 6/3. The answer is _____.
    a. 2
    b. 4
    c. 3.5

2.  Fill in the blank 2 + √5 _____ 7 - √10
    a. >
    b. ≤
    c. ≥

3.  Use division to calculate 50/10. The answer is _____.
    a. 5.5
    b. 8
    c. 5

4.  Which family of numbers begins with the numbers 0, 1, 2, 3, …?
    a. Integers
    b. Whole numbers
    c. Rational numbers

5.  Use division to calculate 7/4. The answer is _____.
    a. 2 R4
    b. 1.5
    c. 1 R3

6.  Which of the answer choices is an INCORRECT statement?
    a. 0 > -1
    b. -2 < -4
    c. 32 < -25x

7.  Simplify: 7 * 5 - 2 + 11
    a. 44
    b. 23
    c. 21

8.  -18 + (-11) = ?
    a. 28
    b. 32
    c. -29

9.  16 - (-7) = ?
    a. 20
    b. 23
    c. 19

10. -12 - (-9) = ?
    a. -3
    b.

11. Simplify: 37 - [5 + {28 - (19 - 7)}]
    a. 16
    b. 36
    c. 46

12. The numbers 1, 2, 3, 4, 5, 6, 7, 8, ........, i.e. natural numbers, are called____.
    a. Positive integers
    b. Rational integers
    c. Simplify numbers

13. _____is the number you are dividing by.
    a. divisor
    b. equation
    c. dividend

14. ____ is the leftover amount when dividend dœsn't divide equally.
    a. remainder
    b. quotient
    c. dividend

# Math: Decimals Place Value

Our basic number system is decimals. The decimal system is built around the number ten. It is sometimes referred to as a base-10 number system. Other systems use different base numbers, such as binary numbers, which use base-2.

The place value is one of the first concepts to grasp when learning about decimals. The position of a digit in a number is represented by its place value. It determines the value of the number.

When the numbers 800, 80, and 8 are compared, the digit "8" has a different value depending on its position within the number.

8 - ones place
80 - tens place
800 - hundreds place

The value of the number is determined by the 8's place value. The value of the number increases by ten times as the location moves to the left.

Select the best answer for each question.

**1.** Which of the following is a decimal number?

    a. 1,852

    b. 1.123

    c. 15

**2.** For the number 125.928, what is in the tenths place?

    a. 9

    b. 2

    c. 5

**3.** For the number 359, which number is in the tens place?

    a. 3

    b. 5

    c. 9

**4.** Write the number 789.1 as an addition problem.

    a. 70 + 800 + 90 + 1

    b. 700 + 80 + 9 + 1 / 10

    c. 700 + 80 + 9+10

**5.** When we say 7 is in the hundreds place in the number 700, this is the same as $7 \times 10^2$.n.

    a. True

    b. False

**6.** For the number 2.14, what digit is in the hundredths place?

    a. 4

    b. 1

    c. 2

**7.** When you start to do arithmetic with decimals, it will be important to_____ properly.

    a. line up the numbers

    b. line up all like numbers

    c. line up numbers ending in 0

**8.** Depending upon the position of a digit in a number, it has a value called its_____.

    a. tenth place

    b. decimals place

    c. place value

**9.** The place value of the digit 6 in the number 1673 is 600 as 6 is in the hundreds place.

    a. True

    b. False

**10.** What is the place value of the digits 2 and 4 in the number 326.471?

    a. 2 is in the tens place. 4 is in the tenths place.

    b. 2 is in the tenths place. 4 is in the tens place.

    c. 2 is in the ones place. 4 is in the tenths place.

# Math: Roman Numerals

The Ancient Romans used Roman numerals as their numbering system. We still use them every now and then. They can be found in the Super Bowl's numbering system, after king's names (King Henry IV), in outlines, and elsewhere. Roman numerals are base 10 or decimal numbers, just like the ones we use today. However, they are not entirely positional, and there is no number zero.

Roman numerals use letters rather than numbers. You must know the following seven letters:

I = 1

V = 5

X = 10

L = 50

C = 100

D = 500

M = 1000

Select the best answer for each question.

1. III = ___
   a. 33
   b. 30
   c. 3

2. XVI=___
   a. 60
   b. 61
   c. 16

3. IV = 5 - 1 =_____
   a. 40
   b. 4
   c. 14

4. What number does the Roman numeral LXXIV represent?
   a. 79
   b. 74
   c. 70

5. Which of the following is the Roman numeral for the number 5?
   a. IV
   b. VI
   c. V

6. How many of the same letters can you put in a row in Roman numerals?
   a. 4 or more
   b. 3
   c. 2

7. Which of the following is the Roman numeral for the number 10?
   a. X
   b. IX
   c. XXI

8. What is the Roman numeral for 33?
   a. XXXIII
   b. XIII
   c. XVIII

9. Which of the following is the Roman numeral for the number 50?
   a. X
   b. L
   c. I

10. Which of the following is the Roman numeral for the number 100?
    a. C
    b. IVV
    c. LII

# Music: Antonio Vivaldi
# Italian Composer

| classical | pianist | Sebastian | performed | red |
|-----------|---------|-----------|-----------|-----|
| orphans | success | death | priest | Venice |

Antonio Vivaldi was a 17th and 18th-century composer who became one of Europe's most famous figures in _____ music.

Antonio Vivaldi was ordained as a _____ but chose to pursue his passion for music instead. He was a prolific composer who wrote hundreds of works, but he was best known for his concertos in the Baroque style, and he was a highly influential innovator in form and pattern. He was also well-known for his operas, such as Argippo and Bajazet.

Antonio Lucio Vivaldi was born in _____, Italy, on March 4, 1678. Giovanni Battista Vivaldi, his father, was a professional violinist who taught his young son to play. Vivaldi met and learned from some of the finest musicians and composers in Venice through his father. While his violin practice flourished, he could not master wind instruments due to chronic shortness of breath.

Vivaldi sought both religious and musical instruction. He began his studies to become a priest when he was 15 years old. In 1703 he was ordained. Vivaldi was known as "il Prete Rosso," or "the Red Priest," because of his _____ hair. Vivaldi's career as a priest was brief. Due to health issues, he could not deliver mass and was forced to resign from the priesthood shortly after his ordination.

At the age of 25, Vivaldi was appointed master of the violin at Venice's Ospedale della Pietà (Devout Hospital of Mercy). In this capacity, he wrote the majority of his major works over a three-decade period. The Ospedale was a school for _____, with the boys learning trades and the girls learning music. The most talented musicians were invited to join an orchestra that performed Vivaldi's compositions, including religious choral music. The orchestra rose to international prominence under Vivaldi's direction. He was promoted to music director in 1716.

Vivaldi's early fame as a composer and musician did not translate into long-term financial _____. After being overshadowed by younger composers and more modern styles, Vivaldi left Venice for Vienna, Austria, possibly hoping to find a position in the imperial court there. Following the _____ of Charles VI, he found himself without a prominent patron and died in poverty in Vienna on July 28, 1741. He was laid to rest in a simple grave following a funeral service devoid of music.

In the early twentieth century, musicians and scholars revived Vivaldi's music, and many of the composer's unknown works were recovered from obscurity. In 1939, Alfredo Casella, a composer, and _____ organized the revival of Vivaldi Week. Since World War II, Vivaldi's music has been widely performed. The choral composition Gloria, which was reintroduced to the public during Casella's Vivaldi Week, is particularly well-known and is regularly _____ at Christmas celebrations worldwide.

Vivaldi's work, which included nearly 500 concertos, influenced later composers such as Johann _____ Bach.

# Nutrition: Reading Labels

Score: _____

Date: _____

Reading food labels can assist you in making educated food choices. Packaged foods and beverages—those in cans, boxes, bottles, jars, and bags—include extensive nutritional and food safety information on their labels or packaging. Keep an eye out for these items on the food label.

On certain foods you purchase, you may notice one of three types of product dates:

"Sell by" indicates how long the manufacturer recommends a store keep foods such as meat, poultry, eggs, or milk products on the shelf—buy them before this date.

The "use by" date indicates how long the food will remain fresh—if you purchase or consume it after that date, some foods may become stale or less tasty.

"Best if used by" (or "best if used before") indicates how long the food will retain its best flavor or quality—it does not suggest a purchase date.

The Food and Drug Administration (FDA) of the United States requires that most packaged foods and beverages bear a Nutrition Facts label. The total number of servings in the container and the food or beverage serving size are listed at the top of the Nutrition Facts label. The serving size indicated on the label is based on the amount of food that most people consume at one time and is not intended to be a guideline for how much to consume.

----------------------------

With permission, read the labels on the containers and answer the questions for each food item. If you do not have any of those items in your home, feel free to find the item online and use that to reference.

## Egg carton

1. What store or farm are they from?

..................................................................................................................................................................

2. Are the eggs free range?

..................................................................................................................................................................

3. Where are the eggs produced or brand?

..................................................................................................................................................................

4. When is the best before date?

..................................................................................................................................................................

5. What is the display date if any?

6. How many calories?

7. Can you recycle the egg carton?

8. How much protein?

9. Should I keep the eggs in the fridge?

10. How many eggs were in the carton?

# Water Bottle

1. What store is the water from and brand?

2. Does the water contains sodium? If so, how much?

3. What is the percent daily value?

4. Can I recycle the bottle?

5. What telephone number should I call if I have a problem?

6. What is the serving size?

7. How many days do I have to drink the water?

# Milk

1. Which store does the milk come from and the brand name?

2. How many pints are in the milk?

3. The milk is ___ _____. A. **Semi-skimmed milk** B. **Whole Milk** C. **Half milk**

4. How much calcium is there?

5. When is the use-by date?

# Juice

1. What store is the juice from?

2. How many **ml** are in one bottle?

3. Can I recycle the bottle?

4. What color is the bottle?

5. Should I keep the juice in the fridge?

# Science Multiple Choice Quiz: Food Chain and Food Web

Score: _____

Date:_____

Select the best answer for each question.

1. In ecology, it is the sequence of transfers of matter and energy in the form of food from organism to organism.
   a. Food Chain
   b. Food Transport
   c. Food Sequencing

2. _____ can increase the total food supply by cutting out one step in the food chain.
   a. Birds
   b. People
   c. Animals

3. Plants, which convert solar energy to food by photosynthesis, are the _____.
   a. secondary food source
   b. tertiary food source
   c. primary food source

4. _____ help us understand how changes to ecosystems affect many different species, both directly and indirectly.
   a. Food Chain
   b. Food Web
   c. Food Transport

5. _____ eat decaying matter and are the ones who help put nutrients back into the soil for plants to eat.
   a. Decomposers
   b. Consumers
   c. Producers

6. _____ are producers because they produce energy for the ecosystem.
   a. Plants
   b. Decomposers
   c. Animals

7. Each organism in an ecosystem occupies a specific _____ in the food chain or web.
   a. trophic level
   b. space
   c. place

8. What do you call an organism that eats both plants and animals?
   a. Herbivores
   b. Carnivores
   c. Omnivores

9. Carnivore is from the Latin words that means _____.
   a. "plant eaters"
   b. "eats both plants and animals"
   c. "flesh devourers"

10. A food web is all of the interactions between the species within a community that involve the transfer of energy through _____.
    a. reservation
    b. consumption
    c. adaptation

11. Why are animals considered consumers?
    a. because they don't produce energy, they just use it up
    b. because they produce energy for the ecosystem
    c. because they only produce energy for themselves

12. How do plants turn sunlight energy into chemical energy?
    a. through the process of photosynthesis
    b. through the process of adaptation
    c. through the process of cancelation

# Science Multiple Choice Quiz:
# Temperate Forest Biome

Score: _____

Date:_____

Select the best answer for each question.

1. _____ are found in Northern Hemisphere regions with moist, warm summers and cold winters, primarily in eastern North America, eastern Asia, and western Europe.
   a. Deciduous forests
   b. Wild forests
   c. Rainforests

2. How many types of forest biomes are there?
   a. 2
   b. 3
   c. 4

3. Temperate forests emerged during the period of global cooling that began at the beginning of the _____.
   a. Medieval Era
   b. Paleozoic Era
   c. Cenozoic Era

4. Major temperate forests are located in the following areas, except for:
   a. Eastern China
   b. Japan
   c. Korea

5. What makes a forest a temperate forest?
   a. Temperature, Two seasons, Tropics, and Clay soil.
   b. Temperature, Climate, Wet season, and Loam soil.
   c. Temperature, Four seasons, Lots of rain, and Fertile soil.

6. The three main types of forest biomes are: the rainforest, the temperate forest, and the _____.
   a. Coniferous
   b. Taiga
   c. Broad-leafed

7. Many trees rely on _____ to get through the winter.
   a. temperature
   b. sap
   c. rain

8. Temperate forests are usually classified into two main groups, and these are: _____ and _____.
   a. Deciduous, Evergreen
   b. Coniferous, Deciduous
   c. Indigenous, Evergreen

9. Deciduous is a Latin word that means _____.
   a. "to rise up"
   b. "to subside"
   c. "to fall off"

10. Certain trees in a temperate forest can grow up to how many feet?
   a. 50 feet tall
   b. 90 feet tall
   c. 100 feet tall

11. _____ forests are made up mostly of conifer trees such as cypress, cedar, redwood, fir, juniper, and pine trees.
   a. Broad-leafed
   b. Mixed coniferous and broad-leafed
   c. Coniferous

12. The animals that live in temperate forests have _____ that allow them to _____ in different kinds of weather.
   a. adaptations, survive
   b. compatibility, survive
   c. conformity, thrive

# Social Skill Interests: Things To Do

A **hobby** is something that a person actively pursues relaxation and enjoyment. On the other hand, a person may have an **interest** in something because they are curious or concerned. Hobbies usually do not provide monetary compensation. However, a person's interests can vary and may lead to earning money or making a living from them. Hobbies are typically pursued in one's spare time or when one is not required to work. Interests can be followed in one's spare time or while working, as in the case of using one's passion as a source of income. A hobby can be a recreational activity that is done regularly in one's spare time. It primarily consists of participating in sports, collecting items and objects, engaging in creative and artistic pursuits, etc. The desire to learn or understand something is referred to as interest. If a person has a strong interest in a subject, he or she may pursue it as a hobby. However, an interest is not always a hobby. Hobbies such as stamp and flower collecting may not be a source of income for a person, but the items collected can sometimes be sold. Hobbies frequently lead to discoveries and inventions. Interests could be a source of income or something done for free. If a person is interested in cooking or enjoys creating dishes, he can do so at home or make it a career by becoming a chef.

_____

*Put the words in the correct category.*

| | | | | | |
|---|---|---|---|---|---|
| pottery | card making | candle making | reading | weaving | knitting |
| gym | jewellery | chess | surfing | computer games | collecting |
| woodwork | Soccer | art | swimming | cooking | skateboarding |
| embroidery | skiing | gardening | writing | chatting | sewing |
| netball | stamp collecting | football | music | rugby | basketball |

| Sport (10) | Handcrafts (10) | Interests (10) |
|---|---|---|
| | | |
| | | |
| | | |
| | | |
| | | |
| | | |
| | | |
| | | |

# Health: Check Your Symptoms

Score: _____

Date: _____

Healthy habits aid in the development of happy and healthy children as well as the prevention of future health issues such as diabetes, hypertension, high cholesterol, heart disease, and cancer.

Chronic diseases and long-term illnesses can be avoided by leading a healthy lifestyle. Self-esteem and self-image are aided by feeling good about yourself and taking care of your health.

**Maintain a consistent exercise schedule.**

No, you don't have to push yourself to go to the gym and do tough workouts, but you should be as active as possible. You can maintain moving by doing simple floor exercises, swimming, or walking. You can also remain moving by doing some domestic chores around the house.

What matters is that you continue to exercise. At least three to five times a week, devote at least twenty to thirty minutes to exercise. Establish a regimen and make sure you get adequate physical activity each day.

**Be mindful of your eating habits.**

You must continue to eat healthily in order to maintain a healthy lifestyle. Eat more fruits and vegetables and have fewer carbs, salt, and harmful fat in your diet. Don't eat junk food or sweets.

Avoid skipping meals since your body will crave more food once you resume eating. Keep in mind that you should burn more calories than you consume.

1. **I've got a pain in my head.**
   a. Stiff neck
   b. headache

2. **I was out in the sun too long.**
   a. Sunburn
   b. Fever

3. **I've got a small itchy lump or bump.**
   a. Rash
   b. Insect bite

4. **I might be having a heart attack.**
   a. Cramps
   b. Chest pain

5. **I've lost my voice.**
   a. Laryngitis
   b. Sore throat

6. **I need to blow my nose a lot.**
   a. Runny nose
   b. Blood Nose

7. **I have an allergy. I have a**
   a. Rash
   b. Insect bite

8. **My shoe rubbed my heel. I have a**
   a. Rash
   b. Blister

9. **The doctor gave me antibiotics. I have a/an**
   a. Infection
   b. Cold

10. **I think I want to vomit. I am**
    a. Nauseous
    b. Bloated

11. **My arm is not broken. It is**
    a. Scratched
    b. Sprained

12. **My arm touched the hot stove. It is**
    a. Burned
    b. Bleeding

13. **I have an upset stomach. I might**
    a. Cough
    b. Vomit

14. **The doctor put plaster on my arm. It is**
    a. Sprained
    b. Broken

15. **If you cut your finger it will**
    a. Burn
    b. Bleed

16. **I hit my hip on a desk. It will**
    a. Burn
    b. Bruise

17. **When you have hay-fever you will**
    a. Sneeze
    b. Wheeze

18. **A sharp knife will**
    a. Scratch
    b. Cut

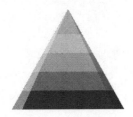

# Art: Roman Portrait Sculptures

| | | | | |
|---|---|---|---|---|
| Alexander | aristocrats | ancestral | shrine | rewarded |
| sculpture | pattern | mosaics | marble | artistic |

Portrait _____ has been practiced since the beginning of Roman history. It was most likely

influenced by the Roman practice of creating _____ images. When a Roman man died, his family

made a wax sculpture of his face and kept it in a special _____ at home. Because these sculptures were

more like records of a person's life than works of art, the emphasis was on realistic detail rather than

_____ beauty.

As Rome became more prosperous and gained access to Greek sculptors, Roman _____

known as patricians began creating these portraits from stone rather than wax.

Roman sculpture was about more than just honoring the dead; it was also about honoring the living. Important

Romans were _____ for their valor or greatness by having statues of themselves erected and

displayed in public. This is one of the earliest of these types of statues that we've discovered, and the

_____ continued all the way until the Republic's demise.

The mosaic is the only form of Roman art that has yet to be discussed. The Romans adored mosaics and created

them with exquisite skill. The Romans created _____ of unprecedented quality and detail using cubes

of naturally colored _____. The floor mosaic depicting _____ the Great at the Battle of

Issus is probably the most famous Roman mosaic.

# Parts of Speech Matching

Score: _____

Date: _____

- **NOUN**. used to identify any of a class of people, places, or things
- **PRONOUN**. a word (such as I, he, she, you, it, we, or they) that is used instead of a noun or noun phrase
- **VERB**. a word used to describe an action, state, or occurrence
- **ADJECTIVE**. modify or describe a noun or a pronoun
- **ADVERB**. word that modifies (describes) a verb (she sings loudly), adverbs often end in -ly
- **PREPOSITION**. word or phrase that connects a noun or pronoun to a verb or adjective in a sentence
- **CONJUNCTION**. word used to join words, phrases, sentences, and clauses
- **INTERJECTION**. word or phrase that expresses something in a sudden or exclamatory way, especially an emotion

|  | |  | |  | |
|---|---|---|---|---|---|
| 1 | ☐ | Identify the noun. | | verb | A |
| 2 | ☐ | Identify the verb. | | mother, truck, banana | B |
| 3 | ☐ | What is an adjective? | | Lion | C |
| 4 | ☐ | Three sets of nouns | | conjunctions | D |
| 5 | ☐ | Three sets of adverbs | | always, beautifully, often | E |
| 6 | ☐ | above, across, against | | a word that describes nouns and pronouns | F |
| 7 | ☐ | but, and, because, although | | preposition | G |
| 8 | ☐ | Wow! Ouch! Hurrah! | | preposition | H |
| 9 | ☐ | Mary and Joe **are** friends. | | barked | I |
| 10 | ☐ | Jane ran **around** the corner yesterday. | | Interjection | J |

**Extra Credit**: Write at least 3 examples of each: Interjection, Conjunction, Adverb & Preposition

_____

_____

_____

# Grammar: Contractions
## Multiple Choice

**Simply put, you replace the letter(s) that were removed from the original words with an apostrophe when you make the contraction.**

**1.** Here is
   a. Here's
   b. Heres'

**2.** One is
   a. Ones'
   b. One's

**3.** I will
   a. Il'l
   b. I'll

**4.** You will
   a. You'll
   b. Yo'ill

**5.** She will
   a. She'll
   b. She'ill

**6.** He will
   a. He'ill
   b. He'll

**7.** It will
   a. It'ill
   b. It'll

**8.** We will
   a. We'll
   b. We'ill

**9.** They will
   a. They'ill
   b. They'll

**10.** That will
   a. That'l
   b. That'll

**11.** There will
   a. There'ill
   b. There'll

**12.** This will
   a. This'll
   b. This'ill

**13.** What will
   a. What'ill
   b. What'll

**14.** Who will
   a. Who'll
   b. Whol'l

# Grammar: Subjunctive Mood

Wishes, proposals, ideas, imagined circumstances, and assertions that are not true are all expressed in the subjunctive mood. The subjunctive is frequently used to indicate an action that a person hopes or wishes to be able to undertake now or in the future. In general, a verb in the subjunctive mood denotes a scenario or state that is a possibility, hope, or want. It expresses a conditional, speculative, or hypothetical sense of a verb.

When verbs of advice or suggestion are used, the subjunctive mood is utilized. After verbs of recommendation or advice, the subjunctive appears in a phrase beginning with the word -that.

Here are a few verbs that are commonly used in the subjunctive mood to recommend or advise.

- advise, ask, demand, prefer

1. Writers use the subjunctive mood to express _____ or _____ conditions.
   a. imaginary or hoped-for
   b.

2. Which is NOT a common marker of the subjunctive mood?
   a.
   b. memories

3. Which is NOT an example of a hope-for verb?
   a. demand
   b. need

4. Subjunctive mood is used to show a situation is not _____.
   a. fictional or fabricated
   b. entirely factual or certain

5. Which of the below statements is written in the subjunctive mood?
   a. I wish I were a millionaire.
   b. What would you do with a million dollars?

6. The indicative mood is used to state facts and opinions, as in:
   a. My mom's fried chicken is my favorite food in the world.
   b. Smells, taste, chew

7. The imperative mood is used to give commands, orders, and instructions, as in:
   a. Eat your salad.
   b. I love salad!

8. The interrogative mood is used to ask a question, as in:
   a. Have you eaten all of your pizza yet?
   b. I ordered 2 slices of pizza.

9. The conditional mood uses the conjunction "if" or "when" to express a condition and its result, as in:
   a. Blue is my favorite color, so I paint with it often.
   b. If I eat too much lasagna, I'll have a stomach ache later.

10. The subjunctive mood is used to express wishes, proposals, suggestions, or imagined situations, as in:
    a. Yesterday was Monday, and I ate pizza.
    b. I prefer that my mom make pasta rather than tuna.

# Biology Vocabulary Words Crossword

Score: _____

Date: _____

**Across**

1. organelle in which photosynthesis takes place
4. a substance used to kill microorganisms and cure infections
5. any substance that stimulates an immune response in the body
6. a chamber connected to other chambers or passageways
8. major ecological community with distinct climate and flora
9. substance that initiates or accelerates a chemical reaction
13. an eyelike marking
15. any toxin that affects neural tissues

**Down**

2. a process in which one substance permeates another
6. any of the forms of a gene that can occupy the same locus
7. a digestive juice secreted by the liver
10. a major division of the vertebrate brain
11. the act of dispersing something
12. the environment as it relates to living organisms
14. that which has mass and occupies space

ATRIUM  BIOME  ANTIGEN
ECOLOGY
CHLOROPLAST  MATTER
ABSORPTION  ANTIBIOTIC
DIFFUSION  ALLELE
EYESPOT  NEUROTOXIN
BILE  CEREBELLUM
CATALYST

# Biology: Reading Comprehension Viruses

When we catch a cold or get the flu, we are dealing with the effects of a viral infection. Viruses, despite sharing some characteristics with living organisms, are neither cellular nor alive. The presence of cells, the ability to reproduce, the ability to use energy, and the ability to respond to the environment are all important characteristics of living organisms. A virus cannot perform any of these functions on its own.

A virus, on the other hand, is a collection of genetic material encased in a protective coat, which is typically made of proteins. Viruses are obligate parasites because they must replicate on the host. To replicate itself, a virus must first attach to and penetrate a host cell, after which it will go through the various stages of viral infection. These stages are essentially the virus lifecycle. A virus can enter the host cell via one of several methods by interacting with the surface of the host cell. The virus can then replicate itself by utilizing the host's energy and metabolism.

Bacteriophages, viruses that infect bacteria, either use the lysogenic cycle, in which the host cell's offspring carry the virus, or the lytic cycle, in which the host cell dies immediately after viral replication. Once viral shedding has occurred, the virus can infect additional hosts. Viral infections can be productive in the sense that they cause active infection in the host, or they can be nonproductive in the sense that they remain dormant within the host. These two types of infection can result in chronic infections, in which the host goes through cycles of illness and remission, as well as latent infections, in which the virus remains dormant for a period of time before causing illness in the host.

1. A virus is encased in a protective coat, which is typically made of _____.
   a. proteins
   b. molecules
   c. cells

2. To replicate itself, a virus must first attach to and penetrate a ___ cell.
   a. healthy
   b. living atom
   c. host

3. Viruses are neither cellular nor __.
   a. alive
   b. moving
   c. a threat

4. The virus can replicate itself by utilizing the host's ___and ___.
   a. cells and DNA
   b. molecules and cell
   c. energy and metabolism

5. A virus can remain _____ for a period of time before causing illness in a host.
   a. metabolized
   b. dormant
   c. infected

# History Reading Comprehension: Storming of the Bastille

Score: _____

Date: _____

| | | | | |
|---|---|---|---|---|
| oppression | fortress | prison | prisoners | fortress |
| military | 1000 | weapons | battle | French |
| assassinated | ruled | commoners | Fearful | craftsmen |

On July 14, 1789, the Bastille was stormed in Paris, France. The _____ Revolution began with a violent attack on the government by the people of France.

During the Hundred Years' War, the Bastille was a _____ built in the late 1300s to protect Paris. By the late 1700s, King Louis XVI had primarily used the Bastille as a state _____.

The majority of the revolutionaries who stormed the Bastille were Paris-based _____ and store owners. They belonged to the Third Estate, a French social class. Approximately _____ men carried out the attack.

The Third Estate had recently made the king's demands, including a more significant say in government for the _____. They were concerned that he was preparing the French army to launch an attack. To arm themselves, they first took over the Hotel des Invalides in Paris to obtain muskets. However, they lacked gun powder. The Bastille was rumored to be full of political _____ and symbolized the king's _____ to many. It also had gunpowder stores, which the revolutionaries required for their _____.

The revolutionaries approached the Bastille on the morning of July 14. They demanded that the Bastille's _____ commander, Governor de Launay, hand over the prison and the gunpowder. He flatly refused. The crowd became agitated as the negotiations dragged on. They were able to gain access to the courtyard in the early afternoon. They began to try to break into the main _____ once they were inside the courtyard. _____ soldiers in the Bastille opened fire on the crowd. The _____ had begun. When some of the soldiers joined the crowd's side, the fight took a turn for the worse. De Launay quickly realized the situation was hopeless. He handed over the fort to the revolutionaries, who took control.

During the fighting, approximately 100 revolutionaries were killed. The crowd _____ Governor de Launay and three of his officers after they surrendered.

The storming of the Bastille triggered a chain of events that culminated in King Louis XVI's deposition and the French Revolution. The revolutionaries' success inspired commoners throughout France to rise up and fight against the nobles who had _____ them for so long.

July 14, the date of the storming of the Bastille, is now celebrated as French National Day. In the same way that the Fourth of July is celebrated in the United States. It is known as "The National Celebration" or "The Fourteenth of July" in France.

Write in your own words, what happened in the storming of the Bastille.

..............................................................................................................................................................

..............................................................................................................................................................

..............................................................................................................................................................

..............................................................................................................................................................

..............................................................................................................................................................

..............................................................................................................................................................

..............................................................................................................................................................

..............................................................................................................................................................

# History Reading Comprehension: The Great Depression

During the 1930s, the United States experienced a severe economic downturn known as the Great Depression. It started in the United States, Wall Street to be exact, but quickly spread throughout the rest of the world. Many people were out of work, hungry, and homeless during this period. People in the city would wait for hours at soup kitchens to get a bite to eat. Farmers struggled in the Midwest, where a severe drought turned the soil into dust, resulting in massive dust storms.

America's "Great Depression" began with a dramatic stock market crash on "Black Thursday," October 24, 1929, when panicked investors who had lost faith in the American economy quickly sold 16 million shares of stock. However, historians and economists attribute the Great Depression to a variety of factors, including drought, overproduction of goods, bank failures, stock speculation, and consumer debt.

When the Great Depression began, Herbert Hoover was President of the United States. Many people held Hoover responsible for the Great Depression. The shantytowns where homeless people lived were even dubbed "Hoovervilles" after him. Franklin D. Roosevelt was elected president in 1933. He promised the American people a "New Deal."

The New Deal was a set of laws, programs, and government agencies enacted to aid the country in its recovery from the Great Depression. Regulations were imposed on the stock market, banks, and businesses as a result of these laws. They assisted in putting people to work and attempted to house and feed the poor. Many of these laws, such as the Social Security Act, are still in effect today.

The Great Depression came to an end with the outbreak of World War II. The wartime economy re-employed many people and filled factories to capacity.

The Great Depression left an indelible imprint on the United States. The New Deal laws expanded the government's role in people's daily lives significantly. In addition, public works improved the country's infrastructure by constructing roads, schools, bridges, parks, and airports.

Between 1929 and 1933, the stock market lost nearly 90% of its value.
During the Great Depression, approximately 11,000 banks failed, leaving many people without savings.

1. The Great Depression began with the _____.
   a. World War II
   b. economy drought
   c. stock market crash

2. Who was President when the Great Depression began?
   a. Herbert Hoover
   b. George W Bush
   c. Franklin D. Roosevelt

3. The New Deal was a set of _____.
   a. laws, programs, and government agencies
   b. city and state funding
   c. stock market bailout

4. The Great Depression came to an end with the outbreak of _____.
   a. new laws
   b. investors funding
   c. World War II

# History: King Tut Reading Comprehension

Tutankhamun was born around 1341 BC as a prince in Egypt's royal court. Pharaoh Akhenaten was his father. Tut was actually born Tutankhaten, but he changed his name after his father died.

Tut was born to one of his father's lesser wives rather than his father's main wife, the powerful Nefertiti. His presence may have caused some tension in the royal courts, as Nefertiti had only daughters and desperately desired to have her own son to succeed to the throne.

Tut's father died when he was seven years old. Tut married his sister (as was common for Pharaohs in Ancient Egypt) and became Pharaoh a few years later. Because he was so young, he needed help ruling the country. Horemheb, a powerful general, and Ay, Tutankhamun's vizier, were the true rulers.

Tutankhamun died when he was about nineteen years old. Archaeologists have no idea what killed him. Some believe he was assassinated, but the most likely cause of death was a leg wound. Scientists discovered that his mummy's leg was broken and infected before he died. This injury was most likely caused by an accident.

Today, Tut is best known for his tomb in the Valley of the Kings. His tomb was most likely built for someone else and was used to bury the young Pharaoh when he died unexpectedly. This may have aided in keeping his tomb hidden from thieves for thousands of years. As a result, when archeologist Howard Carter discovered the tomb in 1922, it was filled with treasure and artifacts not found in any other Pharaoh's tomb.

Did you know that? Lord Carnarvon, Carter's patron (who was best known as the financial backer of the search for and excavation of Tut), died four months after first entering the tomb. Prompting journalists to popularize a "Curse of the Pharaohs," claiming that hieroglyphs on the tomb walls foretold the death of those who disturbed King Tut.

1. **What was King Tut's real name?**
   a. Tutankhaion
   b. Tutankhaten
   c. Tutankhamun

2. **Tut's father died when he was _____ years old.**
   a. 19 yrs old
   b. Twenty-Two
   c. seven

3. **Tutankhamun died when he was about _____ years old.**
   a. nineteen
   b. 16 years old
   c. 21

4. **Nefertiti was the wife of___.**
   a. Tut
   b. Horemheb
   c. Pharaoh Akhenaten

5. **The tomb of young pharaoh Tut is located in the _____.**
   a. Tuts King Egypt
   b. Maine Valley Sons
   c. Valley of the Kings

# Jobs and Careers

Tip: After you've answered the easy ones, go back and work on the harder ones.

| | | | | |
|---|---|---|---|---|
| skill | climbing | monetary | professional | hourly |
| variety | salaried | experience | graduate | achieve |

You might have heard that the education you receive and the information you learn in school will help you get a job when you _____. Or your abilities and skills will benefit you in your future careers. So, what's the truth? How do people decide whether they want a job or a career?

There are several common misconceptions regarding the distinctions between a job and a career. Some people believe that a job is simply an _____ position, whereas a _____ position is a career. Others believe that a career requires a longer educational path that results in exceptional skills and knowledge. The truth is not what most people believe.

A job is a position or set of duties performed for _____ gain, whereas a career is a focused path or journey that a person takes to achieve their professional goals. A career can include a variety of jobs along a career path.

Parents and teachers frequently ask their children what they want to be when they grow up. A career is the answer to that question. A career is a path or _____ journey that a person follows throughout their working life. A career can necessitate extensive education, such as that of a doctor or a lawyer, or it can require extensive _____ training, such as that of an electrician or plumber.

The words "career" and "path" are frequently used interchangeably. A career path is a path that people take to _____ their professional objectives. Many people work for decades on their career paths, which often include a _____ of jobs along the way. With each job, a person gains _____ and skills that will help them get a better job and achieve their career goals.

Another term associated with careers is the concept of people _____ a "career ladder". When people climb the metaphorical career ladder, they progress step by step from one better job to the next. Careers take years to develop and achieve. Sometimes a lot of education is required at the start of a career before a person can start moving up the ladder, whereas other careers require years of experience in the field to get to the top.

# Proofreading Shakespeare: Romeo and Juliet

Score: _____

Date: _____

> There are **24** mistakes in this passage. 5 capitals missing. 3 unnecessary capitals. 4 unnecessary apostrophes. 3 punctuation marks missing or incorrect. 2 incorrect homophones. 7 incorrectly spelled words.

In 1597, William Shakespeare published "Romeo and Juliet" which would go on to become one of the world's most famous love stories. The plot of Shakespeare's pley takes place in Verona, where the two main characters romeo and Juliet, meet and fall in love Both are descended from two feuding families, the Capulets, and the Montagues. As a result, thay choose to keep their luve hidden and are married by Friar Laurence. Romeo gets into a fight with Juliet''s cousin Tybalt, whom he Kills in a Brawl despite his best efforts. Romeo is expelled from Verona and escapes to Mantua.

When juliet's parents press her to marry, she Seeks the assistance of Friar Laurence once more, who provides her with a sleeping potion designed to simulate her death. In a letter that never reaches Romeo, he explains his plan. Disgusted by the alleged death of his beloved Juliet, Rumeo returns to Verona and commits suicide at Juliet's open coffin. Juliet awakens from her slumber, sees what has happened, and decides to end her liphe. The two feuding families now recognize their complicity and reconcile at their children's graves.

The medieval old town of Verona is ideal for putting oneself in the shoes of Romeo and juliet. Every year, many loving couples and tourists come to walk in the footsteps of romeo and Juliet. A photograph of Juliet's famous balcony, a visit to Romeo's home, or sum queit time spent at Julia's grave. No matter were you look in the city, you wall find loving couple's who stick declarations of love and initials on small slips of paper to the walls or immortalize themselve's on the walls or stones of house's - often illegally.

Although Shakespeare's drama never corresponded to reality, verona has a unique charm, especially for lovers, who imagine they can feel the true story behind the literary work, almost as if Romeo and Juliet had really existed.

# Financial: Money, Stocks and Bonds

Score: _____

Date: _____

**Tip:** First, read the entire passage. After that, go back and fill in the blanks. You can skip the blanks you're unsure about and finish them later.

| | | | | |
|---|---|---|---|---|
| prices | obligation | currency | issued | barter |
| stake | coins | exchange | principal | economy |
| profits | piece | conditions | valuable | gold |
| NASDAQ | bankruptcy | golden | services | symbols |
| goods | shareholders | monetary | value | |

Three important _____ must be met in order for something to qualify as a financial asset. It has to be:

Something you can have

Something monetary in nature

A contractual claim provides the basis for that monetary value

That last condition may be difficult to grasp at first, but it will become clear in a few minutes.

As a result, financial assets differ from physical assets such as land or _____. You can touch and feel the actual physical asset with land and gold, but you can only touch and feel something (usually a _____ of paper) that represents the asset of value with financial assets.

Money is a government-defined official medium of _____ that consists of cash and _____.

Money, _____, cash, and legal tender all refer to the same thing. They are all _____ of a central bank's commitment to keep money's value as stable as possible. Money is a financial asset because its value is derived from the faith and credit of the government that issued it, not from the paper or metal on which it is printed.

Money is obviously a _____ financial asset. We would all have to _____ with one another without a common medium of exchange, trading whatever _____ and _____ we have for something else we need, or trade what we have for something else we could then trade with someone else who has what we need. Consider how complicated that can become!

Stock is another crucial financial asset in the US _____. Stock, like money, is simply a piece of paper that represents something of value. The something of value' represented by stock is a _____ in a company. Stock is also known as 'equity' because you have a stake in its _____ when you own stock in a company.

Consider little Jane's lemonade stand as the most basic example. Jane only has $4 to begin her business, but she requires $10. Jane's parents give her $3 in exchange for 30% of her business, a friend gives her $1 for 10%, and her brother gives her $2 in exchange for 20%. Jane, her parents, a friend, and her brother are now all _____ in her company.

That example, as simple as it is, accurately describes stock. The complexities arise when we attempt to assign a _____ value to that stock. A variety of factors determines a stock's _____. One share of stock in one company does not equal one share of stock in another. The number of shares issued by each company, as well as the size and profitability of each company, will affect the value of your share. Anything that has an impact on a business, good or bad, will affect the stock price.

These are the most basic and fundamental factors that can influence the value of a share of stock. Individual stock _____ are affected by macroeconomic trends as well. Thousands of books have been written in an attempt to discover the _____ rule that determines the exact value of a share of stock.

The value of a stock can fluctuate from minute to minute and even second to second. The New York Stock Exchange and _____ were the world's two largest stock exchanges in 2014. (both located in the United States).

Bonds are the final financial asset we'll look at. Bonds are, in essence, loans. When an organization, such as a company, a city or state, or even the federal government, requires funds, bonds can be _____. Bonds come in various forms, but they are all debt instruments in which the bondholder is repaid their _____ investment, plus interest, at some future maturity date.

The only way a bondholder's money is lost is if the entity that issued the bond declares _____. Bonds are generally safer investments than stocks because they are a legal _____ to repay debt, whereas stocks represent ownership, which can make or lose money.

# How It's Made: Money

It's not very often that people think about how the money in their wallets was made or who made it. The federal agency in charge of money creation in the United States is the Department of Treasury. It looks after two branches that make money. The United States Mint produces coins, whereas the United States Bureau of Engraving and Printing produces dollar notes. Let's look at the entire money-making process, from conception to distribution.

Paper money and coin designs are sketched and modeled by designers employed by the United States Department of Treasury. The Secretary of the Treasury selects one of the designs submitted by the designers for production into currency, albeit the final design may be subject to further revisions at this point.

However, why are fresh designs necessary? Technology has made it easier for anyone to create their own counterfeit money. Counterfeiting, the act of creating phony money, is a crime. The government has redesigned our currency to reduce counterfeiting.

Dollar bills and computer paper don't have the same weight and feel. Since paper money is created from a particular cotton and linen blend, it is more difficult to forge. The Bureau of Engraving and Printing also manufactures the ink. Some recent bills (in values of $10 and higher) contain metallic or color-shifting ink to help prevent counterfeiting, which is used on all paper money.

Coins in the United States are created from a combination of metals and alloys. In addition to reducing coin counterfeiting, this usage of bi-metallic elements significantly lowers the cost of minting coins. Coins that are made of pure metal can be worth more than their face value. As a result, instead of utilizing the coins as money, others may opt to melt them and sell the metals they contain.

The Bureau of Engraving and Printing engraves the design onto a plate once it has been created for paper money. The same plate is then replicated numerous times onto a much larger plate that can print multiple bills simultaneously on numerous printers. Ink is applied to the plate, which is then pushed onto the paper. Each side of a sheet of banknotes must dry for 72 hours.

Following the design of the coins, the designs are replicated on stamps that press the design onto the bi-metallic substance. Coins are made from enormous metal sheets, but that's just the beginning. The metal sheets are fed into a machine that punches out coins. Before being stamped with the design, the blank coins are heated and cleaned.

The bills are examined once they've been printed and dried. They remove and discard any bills that have errors. Money that fits the criteria is cut and packaged for distribution. Additionally, the coins are examined, and any that are found to be flawed are disposed of. However, a few of these coins manage to slip through the cracks. When that occurs, the value of these extremely rare coins might skyrocket!

Following an inspection, banks are given the money they require, if needed. After that, the funds are dispersed among the banks' clients. The currency is now in circulation!

Remember, the federal agency in charge of money creation in the United States is the Department of Treasury. The Bureau of Engraving and Printing produces paper currency, whereas the United States Mint produces coins. Numerous safeguards are used during the design, material selection, and production of money to avoid counterfeiting or the production of counterfeit money.

# MONEY

1. The _____ agency is in charge of money creation.
   a. federal
   b. government

2. The United States Mint produces coins and dollar bills.
   a. True - coins and dollar bills
   b. False - only coins

3. Each side of a sheet of banknotes must dry for ___ hours.
   a. 72
   b. 24

4. Dollar bills and computer paper don't have the same _____ and feel.
   a. design
   b. weight

5. The metal sheets are fed into a machine that punches out _____.
   a. coins
   b. silver dollars

6. United States Bureau of _____ produces dollar notes.
   a. Engraving and Printing
   b. Engravers and Commission

7. The Secretary of the _____ selects one of the designs submitted by the designers for production.
   a. Treasury
   b. Bank

8. Coins in the United States are created from a combination of _____.
   a. metals and alloys
   b. silver and nickels

9. Before being stamped with the design, the blank coins are _____.
   a. heated and cleaned
   b. shined and reserved

10. Paper money is created from a particular _____ blend, it is more difficult to forge.
    a. parcel and green dye
    b. cotton and linen

# Introvert vs. Extrovert

Introvert is a person who prefers calm environments, limits social engagement, or embraces a greater than average preference for solitude.

**SYNONYMS:**
brooder
loner
solitary

**Extrovert** is an outgoing, gregarious person who thrives in dynamic environments and seeks to maximize social engagement.

**SYNONYMS:**
character
exhibitionist
show-off
showboat

-------------------------------

Fill in the blank with the correct word. [ introvert, introverts, extrovert, extroverts]

1. Sue is the _____ in the family; opinionated, talkative and passionate about politics.

2. He was described as an _____, a reserved man who spoke little.

3. _____ are often described as the life of the party.

4. An _____ is often thought of as a quiet, reserved, and thoughtful individual.

5. _____ enjoy being around other people and tend to focus on the outside world.

6. Typically _____ tend to enjoy more time to themselves.

7. Jane is an _____ whose only hobby is reading.

8. I am still not as "outgoing" as an _____ is.

9. I had been a very _____ person, living life to the full.

10. I am an _____, I am a loner.

11. Because Pat is an _____ who enjoys chatting with others, she is the ideal talk show host.

12. She is basically an _____, uncomfortable with loud women and confrontations.

# Dealing With Acne

Acne is a skin disorder that results in bumps. Whiteheads, blackheads, pimples, and pus-filled bumps are all sorts of blemishes. What's the source of these annoying bumps? Pores and hair follicles make up most of your skin's top layer. Sebum (pronounced "see-bum"), the natural oil that moisturizes hair and skin, is produced in the pores by oil glands.

Generally, the glands produce adequate sebum, and the pores are good. However, oil, dead skin cells, and bacteria can block a pore if they accumulate in it to an unhealthy level. Acne may result as a result of this.

Puberty-induced hormonal changes are to blame for acne in children. If your parent suffered from acne as a teen, you will likely as well because your pores may produce more sebum when under stress; stress may worsen acne. Acne is usually gone by the time a person reaches their twenties.

**Here are a few tips for preventing breakouts if you suffer from acne:**

- It would help if you washed your face with warm water and a light soap or cleanser in the morning before school and before bed.
- Avoid scrubbing your face. Acne can be exacerbated by irritating the skin, so scrubbing is not recommended.
- Makeup should be washed off at the end of the day if you wear it.
- Ensure to wash your face after a workout if you've been sweating heavily.
- Acne-fighting lotions and creams are readily available over-the-counter. Talk to your parents or doctor about the options available to you.

Make sure you follow the guidelines on any acne medication you use. If you're unsure whether you're allergic to the cream or lotion, use a small amount at first. If you don't notice results the next day, don't give up. Acne medication can take weeks or months to take effect. If you use more than recommended, your skin may become extremely dry and red.

Acne-suffering children can seek treatment from their doctor. Doctors can prescribe stronger medications than what you can get over the counter.

**The following are some other factors to consider:**

- Avoid touching your face if you can.
- Pimples should not be picked, squeezed, or popped.
- Long hair should be kept away from the face, and it should be washed regularly to reduce oil production.

It is possible to get pimples on the hairline by wearing headgear like baseball caps. Stay away from them if you suspect they're contributing to your acne problems.

Despite their best efforts, many children will get acne at some point in their lives. The situation isn't out of the ordinary.

If you suffer from acne, you now have several options for treating it. Remind yourself of this: You are not alone. Take a look around at your buddies and you'll notice that the majority of children and adolescents are dealing with acne, too!

1. Puberty _____ changes are to blame for acne in children.
   a. harmonic
   b. hormonal

2. Pores and hair _____ make up most of your skin's top layer.
   a. follicles
   b. folate

3. Avoid _____ your face.
   a. using cleanser
   b. scrubbing

4. _____ is the oil that moisturizes hair and skin, is produced in the pores by oil glands.
   a. Acne
   b. Sebum

# Smart Ways to Deal With a Bully

Score: _____

Date: _____

First, read over the entire passage(s). Then go back and fill in the blanks. You can skip the blanks you're unsure about and come back to them later.

| | | | | |
|---|---|---|---|---|
| control | popular | confident | ground | society |
| threats | negative | skip | Fighting | mocking |

One of the most serious issues in our _____ today is bullying. It's not uncommon for young people to experience a range of _____ emotions due to this. Bullies may use physical force (such as punches, kicks, or shoves) or verbal abuse (such as calling someone a name, making fun of them, or scaring them) to harm others.

Some examples of bullying include calling someone names, stealing from them and _____ them, or ostracizing them from a group.

Some bullies want to be the center of attention. As a strategy to be _____ or get what they want, they may believe bullying is acceptable. Bullies are usually motivated by a desire to elevate their own status. As a result of picking on someone else, they can feel more power and authority.

Bullies frequently target someone they believe they can _____. Kids who are easily agitated or have difficulty standing up for themselves are likely targets. Getting a strong reaction from someone can give bullies the illusion that they have the power they desire. There are times when bullies pick on someone who is more intelligent than them or who looks different from them somehow.

**Preventing a Bully's Attack**
Do not give in to the bully. Avoid the bully as much as possible. Of course, you aren't allowed to disappear or _____ class. However, if you can escape the bully by taking a different path, do so.

Bravely stand your _____. Scared people aren't usually the most courageous people. Bullies can be stopped by just showing courage in the face of them. Just how do you present yourself as a fearless person? To send a message that says, "Don't mess with me," stand tall. It is much easier to be brave when you are confident in yourself.

**Don't Pay Attention to What the Bully Says or Does.** If you can, do your best not to listen to the bully's _____. Act as though you aren't aware of their presence and immediately go away to a safe place. It's what bullies want: a big reaction to their teasing and being mean. If you don't respond to a bully's actions by pretending you don't notice or care, you may be able to stop them.

**Defend your rights.** Pretend you're _____ and brave. In a loud voice, tell the bully, "No! Stop it!" Then take a step back or even take off running if necessary. No matter what a bully says, say "no" and walk away if it doesn't feel right. If you do what a bully tells you to do, the bully is more likely to keep bullying you; kids who don't stand up for themselves are more likely to be targeted by bullies.

**Don't retaliate by being a bully yourself.** Don't fight back against someone who's bullying you or your pals by punching, kicking, or shoving them. _____ back only makes the bully happier, and it's also risky since someone can be injured. You're also going to be in a lot of trouble. It's essential to stick with your friends, keep safe, and seek adult assistance.

**Inform a responsible adult of the situation.** Telling an adult if you're being bullied is crucial. Find someone you can confide in and tell them what's going on with you. It is up to everyone in the school, from teachers to principals to parents to lunchroom assistants, to stop the bullies. As soon as a teacher discovers the bullying, the bully usually stops because they are worried that their parents will punish them for their behavior. Bullying is terrible, and everyone who is bullied or witnesses bullying should speak up.

# The Human Bones

At birth, a baby's body has about 300 bones. These bones will one day grow together and become the 206 bones that adults have. Some of a baby's bones are made entirely of cartilage, a special material that helps them grow. Other bones in a baby are partially cartilage-covered. This cartilage is soft and easy to move. During childhood, the cartilage grows and is slowly replaced by bone, with the help of calcium, as you get bigger and stronger.

At about 25, this process will be done. Once this occurs, there is no more room for bone growth; the bones have reached their maximum size. There are a lot of bones that make up a skeleton that is both strong and light.

**Spine:** It's easy to look at your spine: When you touch your back, you'll feel bumps on it. The spine lets you twist and bend, and it also keeps your body in place. That's not all: It also helps protect the spinal cord, a long group of nerves that sends information from the brain to the rest of your body. You can't just have one or two bones in your spine. It's made of 33! Vertebrae are the bones that make up the spine, and each one is shaped like a ring.

**Ribs:** Heart, lung, and liver are all essential, and ribs will keep them safe. This makes your chest look like a cage of bones. A few inches below your heart, you can run your fingers along the sides and front of your body to get a sense of the bottom of this cage. It's easy to feel your ribs when you breathe deeply. Some very thin kids can even see some of their ribs through their skin.

**Skull:** The brain is the most important thing in your body, so your skull protects it the best. There are places where you can feel your skull when you push on your head, like in the back a few inches above your neck. Different bones make up the skull. They protect your brain, while other bones make up the shape of your face. If you touch below your eyes, you can feel the bone that makes the hole where your eye goes.

**Arm:** When an arm moves, it connects to a large triangular bone on the upper back corner of each side of the ribcage called a "shoulder blade." You have three bones in your arm: the humerus, which is above your elbow, the radius and ulna, which are below your elbow.

**Pelvis:** The pelvis, a ring of bones at the base of your spine, is where your legs attach. The pelvis, which is like a bowl, holds the spine in place. Large hip bones are in front of the sacrum and coccyx, which are behind. It is made up of the two large hip bones. The pelvis is a hard ring that protects parts of the digestive, urinary, and reproductive systems.

**Joint:** A joint is where two bones meet. This is how some joints work, and some don't: Fixed joints don't move at all. Young people have a lot of these joints in their skulls, called sutures. These joints close up the bones of the skull in their head. One of these joints is called the parieto-temporal suture, which is the one that runs along the side of the skull. It's called this because it connects the two sides of the skull together.

You need to keep your bones healthy. Drinking milk or eating oranges is good for you. They are calcium-rich. Calcium aids in the development of strong bones.

Have you ever suffered from bone fractures? Ouch! A doctor places the bone in its proper position. During the healing process, it is covered in a cast.

The bones of your body are located below the surface of your skin. They can only be seen with an X-ray machine. An X-ray is a type of picture. It allows medical professionals to see if a bone has been broken.

1. **A baby's body has about ____ bones.**
   a. 320
   b. 300

2. **The ____, which is like a bowl, holds the spine in place.**
   a. pelvis
   b. spinal cord

3. **A ____ is where two bones meet.**
   a. legs
   b. joint

4. **At what age is there no more room for growth?**
   a. 25
   b. 18

5. **Adults have how many bones?**
   a. 206
   b. 200

6. **The ____ lets you twist and bend.**
   a. hip bones
   b. spine

7. **Your skull protects your what?**
   a. brain
   b. joints

8. **Your ribs protect your what?**
   a. Heart, spine, and arms
   b. heart, lung, and liver

9. **The ____ connects to a large triangular bone on the upper back corner of each side of the ribcage.**
   a. shoulder blade
   b. joints blade

10. **You have ____ bones in your arm.**
    a. two
    b. three

# US Government: Running for Office

First, read over the entire passage(s). Then go back and fill in the blanks. You can skip the blanks you're unsure about and come back to them later.

| | | | | |
|---|---|---|---|---|
| political | strategy | presidential | government | outlining |
| council | rapport | worries | financial | healthcare |
| requirements | priority | victory | coordinate | memorable |

When running for public office, candidates must persuade voters that they are the best candidate for the position. Running for office is a term for this type of endeavor. Running for office can be a full-time job in some cases, such as the _____ race. When running for office, there are a lot of things to do.

To run for office, the first step is to ensure that you meet all of the _____. For example, one must be at least 18 years of age and a US citizen in order to apply.

Almost everyone joins a political party to run for public office these days. The primary election, in which they run to represent that party, is frequently the first election they must win. The Democratic Party and the Republican Party are the two most influential _____ organizations in the United States today.

Without money, it's challenging to run for office. Candidates frequently use billboards, television commercials, and travel to give speeches to promote their campaigns. All of this comes at a price. The people who want to help a candidate win the election provide them with money. As a result, the budget is established. This is critical, as the person with the most significant _____ resources may be able to sway the greatest number of voters, ultimately leading to their victory.

A candidate's campaign staff should be assembled as well. These are people who will assist the candidate in their bid for the presidency. They _____ volunteers, manage funds, plan events, and generally assist the candidate in winning the election. It is the campaign manager's responsibility to lead the campaign team.

Many candidates attempt to stand out from the crowd by creating a memorable campaign slogan. This is a catchy phrase that will stick in voters' minds as they cast their ballots. Calvin Coolidge and Dwight Eisenhower both had _____ campaign slogans, "I Like Ike" for Eisenhower and "Keep Cool with Coolidge" for Coolidge.

At some point, the candidate will begin a public campaign. A lot of "shaking hands and hugging babies" is involved in the process of running for office. There are a lot of speeches they give _____ what they plan to do when they get into the White House. It's their job to explain why they're better than their rivals.

When a candidate runs for office, they usually take a position on several issues relevant to the position for which they are running. A wide range of topics, such as education, clean water, taxation, war, and _____, are examples.

The debate is yet another aspect of running for office. At a debate, all of the candidates for a particular office sit down together to discuss their positions on a specific issue. Candidates take turns speaking and responding to each other's arguments during the debate. The outcome of a debate between two candidates can mean the difference between

_____ and defeat.

After months of campaigning, the election is finally upon us. They'll cast their ballots and then get right back to work. Attending rallies or shaking hands with strangers on the street may be part of their campaign _____. All the candidates can do is wait until the polls close. Family, friends, and campaign members usually gather to see how things turn out. If they are successful, they are likely to deliver a victory speech and then go to a party to celebrate.

**Becoming Your Class President**

Start working toward your goal of becoming class or high school president as soon as possible if you want to one day hold that position.

If you want to get involved in student _____ your freshman year, go ahead and join, but don't hold your breath waiting to be elected president. Elections for the freshman class council are frequently a complete disaster. Since freshman elections are held within a month of the start of school, no one has had a chance to get to know one another. The person elected president is usually the one whose name has been mentioned the most by other students. A lot of the time, it's not based on competence or trust.

Building trust and _____ with your classmates is essential from the beginning of the school year. This is the most crucial step in the process of becoming a Class Officer President.

Electing someone they like and trust is a top _____ for today's college students. Be a role model for your students. In order to demonstrate your competence, participate in class discussions and get good grades. Avoid being the class clown or the laziest or most absent-minded member of the group.

Become a part of the students' lives. Attend lunch with a variety of people from various backgrounds. Ask them about their _____ and their hopes for the school's future.

Make an effort to attend student _____ meetings even if you aren't currently a member. If you're interested in joining the student council, you may be able to sit in on their meetings, or you may be able to attend an occasional meeting where non-council members can express their concerns and ideas.

# Your Identity and Reputation Online

First, read over the entire passage(s). Then go back and fill in the blanks. You can skip the blanks you're unsure about and come back to them later.

| | | | | |
|---|---|---|---|---|
| persona | remarks | reputation | networking | repercussions |
| embarrassing | real-life | inappropriate | take-backs | derogatory |

Your online identity grows every time you use a social network, send a text, or make a post on a website, for example. Your online _____ may be very different from your real-world persona – the way your friends, parents, and teachers see you.

One of the best things about having an online life is trying on different personas. If you want to change how you act and show up to people, you can. You can also learn more about things that you like. Steps to help you maintain control on the internet can be taken just like in real life.

Here are some things to think about to protect your online identity and reputation:

Nothing is temporary online. The worldwide web is full of opportunities to connect and share with other people. It's also a place with no "_____" or "temporary" situations. It's easy for other people to copy, save, and forward your information even if you delete it.

Add a "private" option for your profiles. Anyone can copy or screen-grab things that you don't want the world to see using social _____ sites. Use caution when using the site's default settings. Each site has its own rules, so read them to ensure you're doing everything you can to keep your information safe.

Keep your passwords safe and change them often. Someone can ruin your _____ by pretending to be you online. The best thing to do is pick passwords that no one can guess. The only people who should know about them are your parents or someone else who you can trust. Your best friend, boyfriend, or girlfriend should not know your passwords.

Don't put up pictures or comments that are _____ or sexually provocative. In the future, things that are funny or cool to you now might not be so cool to someone else, like a teacher or admissions officer. If you don't want your grandmother, coach, or best friend's parents to see it, don't post it. Even on a private page, it could be hacked or copied and sent to someone else.

Don't give in to unwanted advances. There are a lot of inappropriate messages and requests for money that teenagers get when they're on the web. These things can be scary, weird, or even

_____, but they can also be exciting and fun. Do not keep quiet about being bullied online. Tell an adult you trust right away if a stranger or someone you know is bullying you. It's never a good idea to answer. If you respond, you might say something that makes things even worse.

You can go to www.cybertipline.org to report bad behavior or other problems.

Avoid "flaming" by taking a break now and then. Do you want to send an angry text or comment to someone? Relax for a few minutes and realize that the _____ will be there even if you have cooled off or change your mind about them.

People may feel free to write hurtful, _____, or abusive remarks on the internet if they can remain anonymous. We can be painful to others if we share things or make angry comments when we aren't facing someone. If they find out, it could change how they see us. If you wouldn't say it, show it, or do it in person, don't do it online.

Make sure you don't break copyright laws. Don't upload, share, or distribute copyrighted photographs, sounds, or files. Be aware of copyright restrictions. Sharing them is great, but doing so illegally runs the risk of legal _____ down the road.

It's time for a self-evaluation. Take a look at your "digital footprint," which people can find out about you. When you search for your screen name or email address, see what comes up. That's one way to get a sense of what other people think of you online.

In the same way that your _____ identity is formed, your online identity and reputation are also formed. It's different when you're on the internet because you don't always have the chance to explain how you feel or what you mean. Thinking about what you're going to say and being responsible can help you avoid leaving an online trail that you'll later be sorry about.

# Proofreading Interpersonal Skills: Peer Pressure

In this activity, you'll see lots of grammatical *errors*. Correct all the grammar mistakes you see.

> There are **30** mistakes in this passage. 3 capitals missing. 5 unnecessary capitals. 3 unnecessary apostrophes. 6 punctuation marks missing or incorrect. 13 incorrectly spelled words.

Tony is mingling with a large group of what he considers to be the school's cool kids. Suddenly, someone in the group begins mocking Tony's friend Rob, who walks with a limp due to a physical dasability.

They begin to imitate rob's limping and Call him 'lame cripple' and other derogatory terms. Although Tony disapproves of their behavior, he does not want to risk being excluded from the group, and thus joins them in mocking Rob.

Peer pressure is the influence exerted on us by member's of our social group. It can manifest in a variety of ways and can lead to us engaging in behaviors we would not normally consider such as Tony joining in and mocking his friend Rob.

However, peer pressure is not always detrimental. Positive peer pressure can motivate us to make better chioces, such as studying harder, staying in school, or seeking a better job. Whan others influence us to make poor Choices, such as smoking, using illicit drugs, or bullying, we succumb to negative peer pressure. We all desire to belong to a group and fit in, so Developing strategies for resisting peer pressure when necessary can be beneficial.

Tony and his friends are engaging in bullying by moking Rob. Bullying is defined as persistent, unwanted. aggressive behavior directed toward another person. It is moust prevalent in school-aged children but can also aphfect adults. Bullying can take on a variety of forms, including the following:

· Verbil bullying is when someone is called names, threatened, or taunted verbally.
· Bullying is physical in nature - hitting spitting, tripping, or poshing someone.
· Social Bullying is intentionally excluding Someone from activities spreading rumors, or embarrassing sumeone.

· Cyberbullying is the act of verbally or socially bullying someone via the internet, such as through social media sites.

Peer pressure exerts a significant influence on an individual's decision to engage in bullying behavoir. In Tony's case, even though Rob is a friend and tony would never consider mocking his disability, his desire to belong to a group outweighs his willingness to defend his friend

Peer pressure is a strong force that is exerted on us by our social group members. Peer pressure is classified into two types: negative peer pressure, which results in poor decision-making, and positive peer pressure, which influences us to make the correct choices. Adolescents are particularly susceptible to peer pressure because of their desire to fit in

Peer pressure can motivate someone to engage in bullying behaviors such as mocking someone, threatening to harm them, taunting them online, or excluding them from an activity. Each year, bullying affect's an astounding 3.2 million school-aged children. Severil strategies for avoiding peer pressure bullying include the following:

- consider your actions by surrounding yourself with good company.
- Acquiring the ability to say no to someone you trust.

Speak up - bullying is never acceptable and is taken extramely seroiusly in schools and the workplace. If someone is attempting to convince you to bully another person, speaking with a trusted adult such as a teacher, coach, counselor, or coworker can frequently help put thing's into perspective and highlight the issue.

# Proofreading Skills:
# Volunteering

In this activity, you'll see lots of grammatical *errors*. Correct all the grammar mistakes you see.

There are **10** mistakes in this passage. 3 capitals missing. 4 unnecessary capitals. 3 incorrect homophones.

Your own life can be changed and the lives of others, through volunteer work. to cope with the news that there has been a disaster, you can volunteer to help those in need. Even if you can't contribute financially, you can donate you're time instead.

Volunteering is such an integral part of the American culture that many high schools require their students to participate in community service to graduate.

When you volunteer, you have the freedom to choose what you'd like to do and who or what you think is most deserving of your time. Start with these ideas if you need a little inspiration. We've got just a few examples here.

Encourage the growth and development of young people. Volunteer as a Camp counselor, a Big Brother or Big Sister, or an after-school sports program. Special Olympics games and events are excellent opportunities to know children with special needs.

Spend the holidays doing good deeds for others. Volunteer at a food bank or distribute toys to children in need on Thanksgiving Day, and you'll be doing your part to help those in need. your church, temple, mosque, or another place of worship may also require your assistance.

You can visit an animal shelter and play with the Animals. Volunteers are critical to the well-being of shelter animals. (You also get a good workout when you walk rescued dogs.)

Become a member of a political campaign. Its a great way to learn more about the inner workings of politics if your curious about it. If you are not able To cast a ballot, you can still help elect your preferred candidate.

Help save the planet. Join a river preservation group and lend a hand. Participate in a park cleanup day in your community. Not everyone is cut out for the great outdoors; if you can't see yourself hauling trees up a hill, consider working in the park's office or education center instead.

Take an active role in promoting health-related causes. Many of us know someone afflicted with a medical condition (like cancer, HIV, or diabetes, for example). a charity that helps people with a disease, such as delivering meals, raising money, or providing other assistance, can make you Feel good about yourself.

Find a way to combine your favorite things if you have more than one. For example, if you're a fan of kids and have a talent for arts and crafts, consider volunteering at a children's hospital.

People must fill out an application like this or similar before lenders and banks will issue them a credit card or loans.

## Credit Application — PRACTICE ONLY

| Name: | Date Birth: | SSN: |
|---|---|---|

| Current Address: | | Phone: |
|---|---|---|

| City: | State: | ZIP: |
|---|---|---|

| Own    Rent    (Please circle) | Monthly payment or rent: | How long? |
|---|---|---|

| Previous Address: | | |
|---|---|---|

| City: | State: | ZIP: |
|---|---|---|

| Owned  Rented (Please circle) | Monthly payment or rent: | How long? |
|---|---|---|

### Employment Information

| Current Employer: | How long? |
|---|---|

| Employer Address: | Phone: |
|---|---|

| Position: | Hourly   Salary (Please circle) | Annual Income: |
|---|---|---|

| Previous Employer: | |
|---|---|

| Address: | How long? |
|---|---|

| Phone: | E-mail: | Fax: |
|---|---|---|

| Position: | Hourly   Salary  (Please circle) | Annual Income: |
|---|---|---|

| Name and relationship of a relative not living with you: |
|---|

| Address: | | | |
|---|---|---|---|

| City: | State: | ZIP: | Phone: |
|---|---|---|---|

### Co-Applicant Information, if for a joint account

| Name: | Date Birth: | SSN: |
|---|---|---|

| Current Address: | | Phone: |
|---|---|---|

| City: | State: | ZIP: |
|---|---|---|

| Own    Rent    (Please circle) | Monthly payment or rent: | How long? |
|---|---|---|

| Previous Address: | | |
|---|---|---|

| City: | State: | ZIP: |
|---|---|---|

| Owned  Rented (Please circle) | Monthly payment or rent: | How long? |
|---|---|---|

### Employment Information

| Current Employer: | How long? |
|---|---|

| Employer Address: | Phone: |
|---|---|

| Position: | Hourly   Salary  (circle) | Annual Income: |
|---|---|---|

| Previous Employer: | |
|---|---|

| Address: | |
|---|---|

| Phone: | E-mail: | Fax: |
|---|---|---|

| Position: | Hourly   Salary  (circle) | Annual Income: |
|---|---|---|

| Name and relationship of a relative not living with you: |
|---|

| Address: | | | |
|---|---|---|---|

| City: | State: | ZIP: | Phone: |
|---|---|---|---|

### Credit Cards

| Name | Account No. | Current Balance | Monthly Payment |
|---|---|---|---|
| | | | |
| | | | |

### Mortgage Company

| Account No.: | Address: |
|---|---|

### Auto Loans

| Auto Loans | Account No. | Balance | Monthly Payment |
|---|---|---|---|
| | | | |
| | | | |

### Other Loans, Debts, or Obligations

| Description | Account No. | Amount |
|---|---|---|
| | | |
| | | |

### Other Assets or Sources of Income

| | Monthly Value: $ |
|---|---|
| | Monthly Value: $ |

I/We authorize _____ to verify information provided on this form regarding credit and employment history.

| Signature of Applicant | Date |
|---|---|

| Signature of Co-Applicant, if for joint account | Date |
|---|---|

If someone wants to rent an apartment or house, they usually will fill out a document similar to this one here.

| Rental Application | PRACTICE ONLY |
|---|---|

## Applicant information

| Name: | | |
|---|---|---|
| Date of birth: | Ssn: | Phone: |
| Current address: | | |
| City: | State: | ZIP Code: |
| Own    Rent    (Please circle) | Monthly payment or rent: | How long? |
| Previous address: | | |
| City: | State: | ZIP Code: |
| Owned   Rented   (Please circle) | Monthly payment or rent: | How long? |

## Employment information

| **Current employer:** | | |
|---|---|---|
| Employer address: | | How long? |
| Phone: | E-mail: | Fax: |
| City: | State: | ZIP Code: |
| Position: | Hourly    Salary    (Please circle) | Annual income: |

| **Previous employer:** | | |
|---|---|---|
| Address: | | How long? |
| Phone: | E-mail: | Fax: |
| City: | State: | ZIP Code: |
| Position: | Hourly    Salary    (Please circle) | Annual income: |

## Emergency Contact:

| Address: | | Phone: |
|---|---|---|
| City: | State: | ZIP Code: |
| Relationship: | | |

## Credit cards

| Name | Account no. | Current balance | Monthly payment |
|---|---|---|---|
| | | | |
| | | | |
| | | | |
| | | | |

## Auto loans

| Auto loans | Account no. | Balance | Monthly payment |
|---|---|---|---|
| | | | |
| | | | |
| | | | |

# PRACTICE ONLY

This is how some people track their monthly income and expenses. This helps them to plan for how their money will be spent or saved.

| Details of Monthly Expenses | | | | | | | | |
|---|---|---|---|---|---|---|---|---|
| Materials purchased via cash & check | | | | | Other expenses paid via cash & check. | | | |
| Day | Payment made to | Check number | Amount | | Day | Payment made to | Check number | Amount |
| | | | | | | | | |
| | | | | | | | | |
| | | | | | | | | |
| | | | | | | | | |
| | | | | | | | | |
| | | | | | | | | |
| | | | | | | | | |
| | | | | | | | | |
| | | | | | | | | |
| | | | | | | | | |
| | | | | | | | | |
| | | | | | | | | |
| | | | | | | | | |
| | | | | | | | | |
| | | | | | | | | |
| | | | | | | | | |
| | | | | | | | | |
| | | | | | | | | |
| | | | | | | | | |
| | | | | | | | | |
| | | | | | | | | |
| | | | | | | | | |
| | | | | | | | | |
| | | | | | | | | |
| | | | | | | | | |
| | | | | | | | | |
| | | | | | | | | |
| | | | | | | | | |
| | | | | | | | | |
| | | | | | | | | |
| | | | | | | | | |
| Amount Carried Forward | | Reference | | | Amount Carried Forward | | Reference | |
| | | | | | | | | |

# Monthly Budget

| EXPENSE | PLAN | ACTUAL | DIFFERENCE |
|---|---|---|---|
| **HOUSING** | | | |
| Mortgage/Rent | | | |
| Maintenance | | | |
| **UTILITIES** | | | |
| Electric/gas | | | |
| Garbage | | | |
| Water | | | |
| Cable/satellite | | | |
| Internet | | | |
| Phone/cell phone | | | |
| **INSURANCE** | | | |
| Home | | | |
| Automobile | | | |
| Health/life | | | |
| **AUTOMOBILE** | | | |
| Auto payment | | | |
| Fuel | | | |
| Maintenance/repairs | | | |
| Public transportation | | | |
| **FOOD** | | | |
| Groceries | | | |
| Meals out | | | |
| **ENTERTAINMENT** | | | |
| Movie rentals | | | |
| Events | | | |
| Travel | | | |
| **SERVICES** | | | |
| Medical/dental | | | |
| Hair/personal care | | | |
| Other: _____ | | | |
| **MISCELLANEOUS** | | | |
| Clothing | | | |
| Toiletries/cosmetics | | | |
| Cleaning/laundry | | | |
| Pet care | | | |
| Other: _____ | | | |
| **DEBT REPAYMENT** | | | |
| Loans | | | |
| Credit card: _____ | | | |
| Credit card: _____ | | | |
| Other: _____ | | | |
| **CHARITY** | | | |
| **SAVINGS** | | | |
| | | | |
| **Totals:** | | | |

| | | Notes: |
|---|---|---|
| *Monthly income* | | |
| *Planned spending* | | |
| *Actual spending* | | |
| *Over or under amount* | | |

Annual physical exam requirements may vary depending on where you live and school. This form gives you an idea of what info a doctor might share with the school about a student.

## PRIVATE PHYSICIAN'S REPORT OF PHYSICAL EXAMINATION OF A PUPIL OF SCHOOL AGE

DATE _____ 20_____

NAME OF SCHOOL _____ GRADE _____ HOMEROOM _____

NAME OF CHILD

| DATE OF BIRTH | SEX |
| | ☐ ☐ |
| | M  F |

_____
Last                    First                    Middle

ADDRESS

_____
No. and Street    City or Post Office    Borough or Township    County    State    Zip Code

### MEDICAL HISTORY IMMUNIZATIONS AND TESTS

| VACCINE | Enter Month, Day, and Year each immunization was given DOSES | | | BOOSTERS & DATES | |
|---|---|---|---|---|---|
| Diphtheria and Tetanus (Circle): DTaP, DTP, DT, TD | 1 / / | 2 / / | 3 / / | 4 / / | 5 / / |
| Polio (Circle): OPV, IPV | 1 / / | 2 / / | 3 / / | 4 / / | 5 / / |
| Measles, Mumps, Rubella | 1 / / | 2 / / | | | |
| Hepatitis B | 1 / / | 2 / / | 3 / / | | |
| HIB | 1 / / | 2 / / | 3 / / | | |
| Varicella | 1 / / | 2 / / | Varicella Disease or Lab Evidence Date: _____ | | |
| Other: _____ | | | | | |

☐ MEDICAL EXEMPTION  The physical condition of the above named child is such that immunization would endanger life or health
☐ RELIGIOUS EXEMPTION  (Includes a strong moral or ethical conviction similar to a religious belief and requires a written statement from the parent/guardian)

### If Applicable:

| Tuberculin Tests Date Applied | Arm | Device | Antigen | Manufacturer | Signature |
|---|---|---|---|---|---|
| | | | | | |

| Date Read | Results (mm) | Signature |
|---|---|---|
| | | |

Follow-Up of significant tuberculin tests:
Parent/Guardian notified of significant findings on _____.

Result of Diagnostic Studies: _____.
Preventive Anti-Tuberculosis – Chemotherapy ordered.  ☐       ☐      _____
                                                         No      Yes      Date

## Significant Medical Conditions (√)
### If Yes, Explain

|  | Yes | No | |
|---|---|---|---|
| Allergies | ☐ | ☐ | _____ |
| Asthma | ☐ | ☐ | _____ |
| Cardiac | ☐ | ☐ | _____ |
| Chemical Dependency | ☐ | ☐ | _____ |
| Drugs | ☐ | ☐ | _____ |
| Alcohol | ☐ | ☐ | _____ |
| Diabetes Mellitus | ☐ | ☐ | _____ |
| Gastrointestinal Disorder | ☐ | ☐ | _____ |
| Hearing Disorder | ☐ | ☐ | _____ |
| Hypertension | ☐ | ☐ | _____ |
| Neuromuscular Disorder | ☐ | ☐ | _____ |
| Orthopedic Condition | ☐ | ☐ | _____ |
| Respiratory Illness | ☐ | ☐ | _____ |
| Seizure Disorder | ☐ | ☐ | _____ |
| Skin Disorder | ☐ | ☐ | _____ |
| Vision Disorder | ☐ | ☐ | _____ |
| Other (Specify) | ☐ | ☐ | _____ |

Are there any special medical problems or chronic diseases which require restriction of activity, medication or which might affect his/her education?  If so, specify _____

## Report of Physical Examination (√)

| | Normal | Abnormal | Not Examined | Comments |
|---|---|---|---|---|
| Height (inches) | | | | |
| Weight (pounds)  BMI | | | | |
| Pulse (          ) | | | | |
| Blood Pressure | | | | |
| Hair/Scalp | | | | |
| Skin | | | | |
| Eyes/Vision | | | | |
| Ears/Hearing | | | | |
| Nose and Throat | | | | |
| Teeth and Gingiva | | | | |
| Lymph Glands | | | | |
| Heart – Murmur, etc | | | | |
| Lung – Adventitious Finding | | | | |
| Abdomen | | | | |
| Genitourinary | | | | |
| Neuromuscular System | | | | |
| Extremities | | | | |
| Spine (Presence of Scoliosis) | | | | |

_____
**Date of Examination**

_____          _____
**Signature of Examiner**          **PRINT Name of Examiner**

_____          _____
**Address**          **Telephone Number**

When you are a new patient at a clinic, you will likely have to complete a form similar to this.

## Patient Information

### Patient Information

Patient Name: _____ DOB: _____ Sex: _____

Driver's License: _____ SSN: _____

Home Phone: _____ Cell: _____

Address: _____

Employer: _____ Position: _____

Employer Address: _____ Phone No. _____

### Emergency Contact Information

Dependent? _____ If yes, Guardian's Name: _____

Guardian's Phone: _____ Cell: _____

Marital Status: _____ Spouse's Name: _____

Spouse's Employer: _____ Work Phone No. _____

Emergency Contact: _____ Relationship: _____

Home Phone: _____ Cell: _____

Emergency Contact: _____ Relationship: _____

Home Phone: _____ Cell: _____

### Insurance

Insured Party: _____ Relationship to Patient: _____

Insurance Company: _____ Phone No. _____

Address: _____

Policy No. _____ Group No. _____

Dual Coverage? _____ 2$^{nd}$ Insurance Company: _____

Insured Party: _____ Relationship to Patient: _____

Phone No. _____ Address: _____

Policy No. _____ Group No. _____

Payment Method: _____ Card/Check No. _____

I verify that the above information is factual and true to the best of my knowledge. I authorize the doctor to employ X-Rays, photographs, anesthetics, medicines, surgeries, and other equipment or aids as he/she deems necessary in order to provide the proper patient care. I understand that payment, proof of insurance, and/or copay is due at the time of service.

I authorize this office to apply benefits on my behalf for the covered services rendered. I certify that the insurance information I have provided is factual and correct.

_____                    _____
Patient                                                            Date

# Following High School, What Should You Do?

1. Community College offers an _____ degree program.
   - a. bachelors
   - b. associate

2. Many young people take a ___ year to explore their interests and earn money.
   - a. gap
   - b. half

3. If you are between the ages of 16 and 24 and have a low income, you may be eligible for the _____ program.
   - a. Military Program
   - b. Job Corps

4. A vocational or technical school may also be referred to as a secondary school.
   - a. False - trade school
   - b. True - secondary or post-school

5. Community College offers an associate degree program.
   - a. True
   - b. False

6. To earn a bachelor's degree, students must attend a _____ college or university.
   - a. two-year
   - b. four-year

# My First Resume

When you're a high school student, writing a résumé can be __intimidating__. The good news is that you probably have more work experience than you realize, even if this is your first résumé. Experiences such as childcare, yard work, and volunteerism all __contribute__ to developing key work skills that companies seek. Simply because you have not held a position similar to the one you are seeking does not indicate you lack the requisite abilities to succeed.

Be sure to include any previous employment, especially if it was for pay. Other than that, you can consist of informal work such as pet sitting, cutting grass, snow shoveling, and any other tasks you've done for money. Although you may not have received a __regular__ income for your informal employment, your talents and reliability as an employee can still be shown via it.

Given that the majority of teenagers have not held many jobs, it is critical to draw on all elements of your life that prove you possess the attitude, willingness to work hard, competencies, and personality necessary for job success.

Please list any __leadership__ positions you held (for example, a president of an organization or as team captain), as well as any honors or awards you have received. Include a list of your duties and accomplishments under each heading.

Employers are more concerned with your work __habits__ and attitude than anything else. Nobody expects you to be an expert in your field. When recounting an experience, you might use language to the effect that you have perfect or near-perfect attendance and are on time for school and other commitments.

Employers are looking for employees who have a history of positively impacting the company. Ask yourself whether there are any accomplishments that you can include from your time in school, your clubs, or your employment. Use verbs like "upgraded," "started," and "expanded" to describe what you've done if you want to illustrate what you've accomplished. To demonstrate to __potential__ employers that you are both bright and ambitious, include any demanding advanced academic assignments on your resume.

Keep it short: Keep it simple (But Include All Necessary Information). A single page is all you need. Contact information and previous work experience are both required in some way on every resume. On the other hand, you can exclude things like a career objective or summary.

Create a narrative. Match your talents and expertise to the job's requirements. For example, in the case of a cashier position, if you've never had a position with that precise title before, emphasize your customer service abilities, aptitude for mathematical calculations, work ethic, and ability to operate as part of a team. Examine the job description and make sure your __qualifications__ meet the requirements.

It is also appropriate to add information about your academic achievements, such as participation in organizations and the necessary curriculum you finished while producing a college __freshman__ resume or a resume for a college application. Suppose you're applying for work as a front desk receptionist at a hotel. You could want to include the talents you gained while studying hospitality at a school.

Finally, be sure to double- or even triple-check your resume for typos and __grammatical__ errors. You may be tempted to send in your resume as soon as you finish it, but take a few minutes to review it.

As a last resort, ask for a second opinion on your resume from friends, family, or school teachers. Have them go it through to see if there's anything you missed or if you can make any __improvements__.

# Test Your Mathematics
# Knowledge

**1.** To add fractions_____
- a. the denominators must be the same
- b. the denominators can be same or different
- c. the denominators must be different

**2.** To add decimals, the decimal points must be?
- a. column and carry the first digit(s)
- b. lined up in any order before you add the columns
- c. lined up vertically before you add the columns

**3.** When adding like terms_____
- a. the like terms must be same and they must be to the different power.
- b. the exponent must be different and they must be to the same power.
- c. the variable(s) must be the same and they must be to the same power.

**4.** The concept of math regrouping involves_____
- a. regrouping means that 5x + 2 becomes 50 + 12
- b. the numbers you are adding come out to five digit numbers and 0
- c. rearranging, or renaming, groups in place value

**5.** _____ indicates how many times a number, or algebraic expression, should be multiplied by itself.
- a. Denominators
- b. Division-quotient
- c. Exponent

**6.** _____ is the numerical value of a number without its plus or minus sign.
- a. Absolute value
- b. Average
- c. Supplementary

**7.** Any number that is less than zero is called_____
- a. Least common multiple
- b. Equation
- c. Negative number

**8.** $2^3 = 2 \times 2 \times 2 = 8$, 8 is the
- a. third power of 2
- b. first power of 2
- c. second power of 2

**9.** -7, 0, 3, and 7.12223 are
- a. all real numbers
- b. all like fractions
- c. all like terms

**10.** How do you calculate 2 + 3 x 7?
- a. $2 + 3 \times 7 = 2 + 21 = 23$
- b. $2 + 7 \times 7 = 2 + 21 = 35$
- c. $2 + 7 \times 3 = 2 + 21 = 23$

**11.** How do you calculate (2 + 3) x (7 - 3)?

    a. (2 + 2) x (7 - 3) = 5 x 4 = 32

    b. [ (2 + 3) x (7 - 3) = 5 x 4 = 20 ]

    c. (2 + 7) x (2 - 3) = 5 x 4 = 14

**12.** The Commutative Law of Addition says_____

    a. positive - positive = (add) positive

    b. [ that it doesn't matter what order you add up numbers, you will always get the same answer ]

    c. parts of a calculation outside brackets always come first

**13.** The Zero Properties Law of multiplication says_____

    a. [ that any number multiplied by 0 equals 0 ]

    b. mathematical operation where four or more numbers are combined to make a sum

    c. Negative - Positive = Subtract

**14.** Multiplication is when you_____

    a. numbers that are added together in multiplication problems

    b. [ take one number and add it together a number of times ]

    c. factor that is shared by two or more numbers

**15.** When multiplying by 0, the answer is always_____

    a. [ 0 ]

    b. [ -0 ]

    c. 1

**16.** When multiplying by 1, the answer is always the _____

    a. same as the number multiplied by 0

    b. same as the number multiplied by -1

    c. [ same as the number multiplied by 1 ]

**17.** You can multiply numbers in_____

    a. any order and multiply by 2 and the answer will be the same

    b. [ any order you want and the answer will be the same ]

    c. any order from greater to less than and the answer will be the same

**18.** Division is____

    a. set of numbers that are multiplied together to get an answer

    b. [ breaking a number up into an equal number of parts ]

    c. division is scaling one number by another

**19.** If you take 20 things and put them into four equal sized groups

    a. there will be 6 things in each group

    b. [ there will be 5 things in each group ]

    c. there will be 10 things in each group

**20.** The dividend is_____

    a. the number you are multiplied by

    b. [ the number you are dividing up ]

    c. the number you are grouping together

**21.** The divisor is _____

    a. are all multiples of 3

    b. [ the number you are dividing by ]

    c. common factor of two numbers

**22.** The quotient is _____

    a. [ the answer ]

    b. answer to a multiplication operation

    c. any number in the problem

**23.** When dividing something by 1_____

    a. the answer is the original number

    b. the answer produces a given number when multiplied by itself

    c. the answer is the quotient

**24.** Dividing by 0_____

    a. the answer will always be more than 0

    b. You will always get 1

    c. You cannot divide a number by 0

**25.** If the answer to a division problem is not a whole number, the number(s) leftover_____

    a. are called the Order Property

    b. are called the denominators

    c. are called the remainder

**26.** You can figure out the 'mean' by_____

    a. multiply by the sum of two or more numbers

    b. adding up all the numbers in the data and then dividing by the number of numbers

    c. changing the grouping of numbers that are added together

**27.** The 'median' is the_____

    a. last number of the data set

    b. middle number of the data set

    c. first number of the data set

**28.** The 'mode' is the number_____

    a. that appears equal times

    b. that appears the least

    c. that appears the most

**29.** Range is the_____

    a. difference between the less than equal to number and the highest number.

    b. difference between the highest number and the highest number.

    c. difference between the lowest number and the highest number

**30.** Please Excuse My Dear Aunt Sally: What it means in the Order of Operations is_____

    a. Parentheses, Exponents, Multiplication and Division, and Addition and Subtraction

    b. Parentheses, Equal, Multiplication and Decimal, and Addition and Subtraction

    c. Parentheses, Ellipse, Multiplication and Data, and Addition and Subtraction

**31.** A ratio is_____

    a. a way to show a relationship or compare two numbers of the same kind

    b. short way of saying that you want to multiply something by itself

    c. he sum of the relationship a times x, a times y, and a times z

**32.** Variables are things_____

    a. that can change or have different values

    b. when something has an exponent

    c. the simplest form using fractions

**33.** Always perform the same operation to_____ of the equation.

    a. when the sum is less than the operation

    b. both sides

    c. one side only

**34.** The slope intercept form uses the following equation:

    a. $y = mx + b$

    b. $y = x + ab$

    c. $x = mx + c$

**35.** The point-slope form uses the following equation:

    a. $y - y1 = m(y - x2)$

    b. $y - y1 = m(x - x1)$

    c. $x - y2 = m(x - x1)$

**36.** Numbers in an algebraic expression that are not variables are called____

    a. Square

    b. Coefficient

    c. Proportional

**37.** A coordinate system is _____

    a. a type of cubed square

    b. a coordinate reduced to another proportion plane

    c. a two-dimensional number line

**38.** Horizontal axis is called_____

    a. h-axis

    b. x-axis

    c. y-axis

**39.** Vertical axis is called____

    a. v-axis

    b. y-axis

    c. x-axis

**40.** Equations and inequalities are both mathematical sentences____

    a. has y and x variables as points on a graph

    b. reduced ratios to their simplest form using fractions

    c. formed by relating two expressions to each other

# Geography: Time Zones

Have you ever tried to call or send a  message  to someone who was on the other side of the country or the world? It can be tough to reach a faraway location from you because the time of  day  may be different from your own. The purpose of time zones and why we have them will be discussed in this session.

Kim, Mike's  classmate  who recently relocated across the country, is texting him. After a short time, Kim sends Mike a text message saying that it is time for her to go to sleep for the night. The sun is beaming brightly  outside , and Mike is confused about why Kim would choose this time of day to go to sleep. 'Can you tell me what  time  it is, please?' Mike asked. 'It's 9:00 p.m. now!' Kim replies.

What exactly is going on here? Was Mike able to travel back in time in some way?

What is happening to Mike and Kim is nothing more than a natural occurrence that occurs on our planet daily. Since Kim relocated across the country, she is now in a  different  time zone than she was previously.

A time zone is a geographical location on the planet with a fixed time that all citizens can observe by setting their clocks  to that time. As you go from east to west (or west to east) on the globe's surface, you will encounter different time zones. The greater the distance traveled, the greater the number of time zones crossed.

Time zones are not something that arises in nature by chance. Humans created the concept of time zones and determined which regions of the world are located in which time zones.

Because of time zones, everyone experiences the same pattern of dawn in the early morning and sunset in the late afternoon. We require time zones because the earth is shaped like a  ball  and therefore requires them. As the sun beams down on the planet, not every location receives the same amount of sunshine. The sun  shines  on one side of the earth and brightens it during the day, while the other side is dark during the night (nighttime). If time-zones didn't  exist , many people worldwide would experience quite strange sunshine patterns during the day if there were no time zones.

# Science: Albert Einstein

Albert Einstein was born in __Germany__ on March 14, 1879. Because he was Jewish, he fled to the United States to avoid Hitler and the Second World War.

His father gave him a simple __pocket__ compass when he was about five years old, and it quickly became his favorite toy!

He developed an interest in __mathematics__ and science at the age of seven.

When Einstein was about ten years old, a much older friend gave him a large stack of science, mathematics, and philosophy __books__.

He'd published his first scientific __paper__ by the age of sixteen. That is absolutely incredible!

Numerous reports have shown that Einstein __failed__ math in school, but his family has stated that this is not the case. They claimed he was always at the __top__ of his class in math and could solve some challenging problems.

As an adult, he frequently __missed__ appointments, and because his mind was all over the place, his lectures were a little difficult to understand.

He didn't wear __socks__ and had uncombed hair! Even at posh dinners, he'd arrive unkempt, with crumpled clothes and, of course, no socks!

An __experiment__ in 1919 proved the theory correct. He became famous almost __overnight__, and he suddenly received invitations to travel worldwide, as well as honors from all over the world!

In 1921, he was awarded the __Nobel__ Prize for Physics. He'd come a long way from the boy who was told he'd never amount to anything!

Today, his other discoveries enabled us to have things like garage __door__ openers, televisions, and DVD players. Time magazine named him "Person of the Century" in 1999.

One of his favorite activities was to take a __boat__ out on a lake and take his notebook with him to think and write everything down. Perhaps this is what inspired him to create his inventions!

Einstein's first __marriage__ produced two sons. His daughter, Lierserl, is believed to have died when she was young. He married twice, and she died before him.

# Government History: How Laws Are Made

1. If the Senate approves the bill, it will be sent to the _____.
   a. President
   b. House Representee

2. The _____ may decide to make changes to the bill before it is passed.
   a. governor
   b. committee

3. The bill must then be _____ by a member of Congress.
   a. signed
   b. sponsored

4. The President has the option of refusing to sign the bill. This is known as a ___.
   a. voted
   b. veto

5. The Senate and House can choose to override the President's veto by ____again.
   a. creating a new bill
   b. voting

6. The bill is assigned to a committee after it is _____.
   a. introduced
   b. vetoed

7. Bills are created and passed by ____.
   a. The House
   b. Congress

8. A bill must be signed into law by the President within ___-days.
   a. 10
   b. 5

9. The President's ____ is the final step in a bill becoming law.
   a. signature
   b. saying yes

10. If the committee agrees to pass the bill, it will be sent to the House or Senate's main ___ for approval.
    a. chamber
    b. state

Extra Credit: What are some of the weirdest laws in the world? List at least 5. (Independent student's answers)

[Student worksheet has a 19 line writing exercise here.]

# History: United States Armed Forces

1. The United States military is divided into ___ branches.
   a. [ six ]
   b. five

2. _____ is managed by the United States Department of Homeland Security.
   a. The National Guard
   b. [ The Coast Guard ]

3. The _____ of the United States is the Commander in Chief of the United States Armed Forces.
   a. Governor
   b. [ President ]

4. The United States maintains a military to safeguard its _____ and interests.
   a. [ borders ]
   b. cities

5. DoD is in charge of controlling each _____ of the military.
   a. [ branch ]
   b. army

6. The Marines are prepared to fight on both land and ____.
   a. battlefield
   b. [ sea ]

7. The United States Space Force is in charge of operating and defending military _____ and ground stations.
   a. soldiers
   b. [ satellites ]

8. The mission of the _____ is to defend the country from outside forces.
   a. United States DoD Forces
   b. [ United States Air Force ]

9. There are _____ units in all 50 states.
   a. [ Army National Guard ]
   b. Armed Nations Guard

10. The United States Navy conducts its missions at sea to secure and protect the world's _____.
    a. [ oceans ]
    b. borders

11. The primary concern of the United States Coast Guard is to protect_____.
    a. [ domestic waterways ]
    b. domesticated cities

12. The United States military is: the Amy Force, Army, Coast Guard, Mario Corps, Old Navy, and Space Force.
    a. True
    b. [ False ]

Extra Credit:  Has America ever been invaded? (Independent student research answer)

[Student worksheet has a 19 line writing exercise here.]

# Grammar: Adjectives Matching

Adjectives are words that describe people, places, and things, or nouns. Adjectives are words that describe sounds, shapes, sizes, times, numbers/quantity, textures/touch, and weather. You can remember this by saying to yourself, "an adjective adds something."

If you need to describe a friend or an adult, you can use words that describe their appearance, size, or age. When possible, try to use positive words that describe a person.

| 1 | O | disappointed | ⇢ | sad because something is worse than expected |
| 2 | K | anxious | ⇢ | worried |
| 3 | C | delighted | ⇢ | very pleased |
| 4 | G | terrified | ⇢ | very frightened |
| 5 | I | ashamed | ⇢ | feeling bad because you did sg wrong |
| 6 | H | envious | ⇢ | wanting something another person has |
| 7 | N | proud | ⇢ | feeling pleased and satisfied |
| 8 | F | shocked | ⇢ | very surprised and upset |
| 9 | A | brave | ⇢ | nothing frightens him/her |
| 10 | L | hard-working | ⇢ | has 2 or more jobs |
| 11 | B | organized | ⇢ | everything is in order around him |
| 12 | D | punctual | ⇢ | always arrives in time |
| 13 | J | honest | ⇢ | uprightness and fairness |
| 14 | E | outgoing | ⇢ | loves being with people |
| 15 | M | loyal | ⇢ | always supports his friends |
| 16 | P | reliable | ⇢ | one can always count on him |

# History: The Thirteen Colonies

1. **The Dutch founded _____ in 1626.**
   a. New Jersey
   b. New York

2. **13 British colonies merged to form the_____.**
   a. United Kingdom
   b. United States

3. **Roger Williams founded _____.**
   a. Maryland
   b. Rhode Island

4. **A colony is a region of _____ that is politically controlled by another country.**
   a. land
   b. township

5. **Middle Colonies:**
   a. Delaware, New Jersey, New York, Pennsylvania
   b. Georgia, Maryland, North Carolina, South Carolina, Texas

6. **Colonies are typically founded and settled by people from the ___ country.**
   a. home
   b. outside

7. **Southern Colonies:**
   a. Maine, New Jersey, New York, Pennsylvania
   b. Georgia, Maryland, North Carolina, South Carolina, Virginia

8. **Many of the colonies were established by ____leaders or groups seeking religious liberty.**
   a. political
   b. religious

9. **New England Colonies:**
   a. Connecticut, Massachusetts Bay, New Hampshire, Rhode Island
   b. Ohio, Tennessee, New York, Pennsylvania

10. **George and Cecil Calvert established _____ as a safe haven for Catholics.**
    a. Maine
    b. Maryland

11. **The colonies are frequently divided into_____.**
    a. New England Colonies, Middle Colonies, and Southern Colonies
    b. United England Colonies, Midland Colonies, and Southern Colonies.

# Confusing Vocab Words

1. He __accepts__ [ accepts / accept / excepts ] defeat well.

2. Please take all the books off the table __except__ [ exception / accept / except ] for the thick one.

3. Lack of sleep __affects__ [ affects / affect / effect ] the quality of your work.

4. The __effect__ [ effects / affect / effect ] of the light made the room bright.

5. I have a __lot__ [ alot / lot / lots ] of friends.

6. The magician preformed a great __illusion__ [ illusion / allusion / trick ] .

7. Dinner was all __ready__ [ already / good / ready ] when the guests arrived.

8. The turkey was __already__ [ al ready / already / all ready ] cooked when the guests arrived.

9. __Altogether__ [ All together / Altogether / altogether ] , I thought it was a great idea!

10. We were all __together__ [ altogether / group / together ] at the family reunion.

11. The fence kept the dogs __apart__ [ apart / a part / parted ] .

12. A __part__ [ section / part / Apart ] of the plan is to wake up at dawn.

13. The plane's __ascent__ [ assent / descent / ascent ] made my ears pop.

14. You could see his __breath__ [ breath / breathing / breathe ] in the cold air.

15. If you don't __breathe__ [ breath / breathe / breathing ] , then you are dead.

16. The __capital__ [ capital / capitol / city ] of Hawaii is Honolulu.

17. That is the __capitol__ [ capital / capitol / captain ] building.

18. I __cited__ [ sighted / sited / cited ] 10 quotes from the speech.

19. You can not build on that __site__ [ cite / sight / site ] .

20. The __sight__ [ cite / site / sight ] of land is refreshing.

21. I **complimented** [ complimented / complemented / discouraged ] my wife on her cooking.

22. We all have a **conscience** [ conscience / mind / conscious ] of right and wrong.

23. The boxer is still **conscious** [ conscience / conscious / knocked out ] .

24. I went to the city **council** [ municipal / counsel / council ] meeting.

25. My accountant **counseled** [ directed / counciled / counseled ] me on spending habits.

26. The teacher **elicited** [ brought out / illicit / elicited ] the correct response.

27. The criminal was arrested for **illicit** [ elicit / illicit / illegal ] activities.

28. The baby will cry as soon as **its** [ its' / it's / its ] mother leaves.

29. **It's** [ It's / It is / Its ] a beautiful day

30. I have a headache, so I'm going to **lie** [ lay / lain / lie ] down.

31. You should never tell a **lie** [ lay / lie / lye ] .

32. If you **lose** [ lose / find / loose ] your phone, I will not buy a new one!

33. My pants feel **loose** [ loose / tight / lose ] , I need a belt.

34. I **kind** [ kindly / kind / a bit ] of like spicy food.

35. He is a very **kind** [ kind of / mean / kind ] teacher.

# Math: Arithmetic Refresher

Select the best answer for each question.

**1.** Use division to calculate 6/3. The answer is _____.
- a. 2
- b. 4
- c. 3.5

**2.** Fill in the blank 2 + √5 _____ 7 - √10
- a. >
- b. ≤
- c. ≥

**3.** Use division to calculate 50/10. The answer is _____.
- a. 5.5
- b. 8
- c. 5

**4.** Which family of numbers begins with the numbers 0, 1, 2, 3, …?
- a. Integers
- b. Whole numbers
- c. Rational numbers

**5.** Use division to calculate 7/4. The answer is _____.
- a. 2 R4
- b. 1.5
- c. 1 R3

**6.** Which of the answer choices is an INCORRECT statement?
- a. 0 > -1
- b. -2 < -4
- c. 32 < -25x

**7.** Simplify: 7 * 5 - 2 + 11
- a. 44
- b. 23
- c. 21

**8.** -18 + (-11) = ?
- a. 28
- b. 32
- c. -29

**9.** 16 - (-7) = ?
- a. 20
- b. 23
- c. 19

**10.** -12 - (-9) = ?
- a. -3
- b.

**11.** Simplify: 37 - [5 + {28 - (19 - 7)}]
- a. 16
- b. 36
- c. 46

**12.** The numbers 1, 2, 3, 4, 5, 6, 7, 8, ........, i.e. natural numbers, are called____.
- a. Positive integers
- b. Rational integers
- c. Simplify numbers

**13.** _____is the number you are dividing by.
- a. divisor
- b. equation
- c. dividend

**14.** ____ is the leftover amount when dividend doesn't divide equally.
- a. remainder
- b. quotient
- c. dividend

# Math: Decimals Place Value

Our basic number system is decimals. The decimal system is built around the number ten. It is sometimes referred to as a base-10 number system. Other systems use different base numbers, such as binary numbers, which use base-2.

The place value is one of the first concepts to grasp when learning about decimals. The position of a digit in a number is represented by its place value. It determines the value of the number.

When the numbers 800, 80, and 8 are compared, the digit "8" has a different value depending on its position within the number.

8 - ones place
80 - tens place
800 - hundreds place

The value of the number is determined by the 8's place value. The value of the number increases by ten times as the location moves to the left.

Select the best answer for each question.

1. Which of the following is a decimal number?
   a. 1,852
   b. 1.123
   c. 15

2. For the number 125.928, what is in the tenths place?
   a. 9
   b. 2
   c. 5

3. For the number 359, which number is in the tens place?
   a. 3
   b. 5
   c. 9

4. Write the number 789.1 as an addition problem.
   a. 70 + 800 + 90 + 1
   b. 700 + 80 + 9 + 1 / 10
   c. 700 + 80 + 9+10

5. When we say 7 is in the hundreds place in the number 700, this is the same as 7x10$^2$.n.
   a. True
   b. False

6. For the number 2.14, what digit is in the hundredths place?
   a. 4
   b. 1
   c. 2

7. When you start to do arithmetic with decimals, it will be important to_____ properly.
   a. line up the numbers
   b. line up all like numbers
   c. line up numbers ending in 0

8. Depending upon the position of a digit in a number, it has a value called its_____.
   a. tenth place
   b. decimals place
   c. place value

9. The place value of the digit 6 in the number 1673 is 600 as 6 is in the hundreds place.
   a. True
   b. False

10. What is the place value of the digits 2 and 4 in the number 326.471?
    a. 2 is in the tens place. 4 is in the tenths place.
    b. 2 is in the tenths place. 4 is in the tens place.
    c. 2 is in the ones place. 4 is in the tenths place.

# Math: Roman Numerals

The Ancient Romans used Roman numerals as their numbering system. We still use them every now and then. They can be found in the Super Bowl's numbering system, after king's names (King Henry IV), in outlines, and elsewhere. Roman numerals are base 10 or decimal numbers, just like the ones we use today. However, they are not entirely positional, and there is no number zero.

Roman numerals use letters rather than numbers. You must know the following seven letters:

I = 1

V = 5

X = 10

L = 50

C = 100

D = 500

M = 1000

Select the best answer for each question.

**1.** III = ___
   a. 33
   b. 30
   c. 3

**2.** XVI=___
   a. 60
   b. 61
   c. 16

**3.** IV = 5 - 1 =____
   a. 40
   b. 4
   c. 14

**4.** What number does the Roman numeral LXXIV represent?
   a. 79
   b. 74
   c. 70

**5.** Which of the following is the Roman numeral for the number 5?
   a. IV
   b. VI
   c. V

**6.** How many of the same letters can you put in a row in Roman numerals?
   a. 4 or more
   b. 3
   c. 2

**7.** Which of the following is the Roman numeral for the number 10?
   a. X
   b. IX
   c. XXI

**8.** What is the Roman numeral for 33?
   a. XXXIII
   b. XIII
   c. XVIII

**9.** Which of the following is the Roman numeral for the number 50?
   a. X
   b. L
   c. I

**10.** Which of the following is the Roman numeral for the number 100?
   a. C
   b. IVV
   c. LII

# Music: Antonio Vivaldi
# Italian Composer

Antonio Vivaldi was a 17th and 18th-century composer who became one of Europe's most famous figures in __classical__ music.

Antonio Vivaldi was ordained as a __priest__ but chose to pursue his passion for music instead. He was a prolific composer who wrote hundreds of works, but he was best known for his concertos in the Baroque style, and he was a highly influential innovator in form and pattern. He was also well-known for his operas, such as Argippo and Bajazet.

Antonio Lucio Vivaldi was born in __Venice__, Italy, on March 4, 1678. Giovanni Battista Vivaldi, his father, was a professional violinist who taught his young son to play. Vivaldi met and learned from some of the finest musicians and composers in Venice through his father. While his violin practice flourished, he could not master wind instruments due to chronic shortness of breath.

Vivaldi sought both religious and musical instruction. He began his studies to become a priest when he was 15 years old. In 1703 he was ordained. Vivaldi was known as "il Prete Rosso," or "the Red Priest," because of his __red__ hair. Vivaldi's career as a priest was brief. Due to health issues, he could not deliver mass and was forced to resign from the priesthood shortly after his ordination.

At the age of 25, Vivaldi was appointed master of the violin at Venice's Ospedale della Pietà (Devout Hospital of Mercy). In this capacity, he wrote the majority of his major works over a three-decade period. The Ospedale was a school for __orphans__, with the boys learning trades and the girls learning music. The most talented musicians were invited to join an orchestra that performed Vivaldi's compositions, including religious choral music. The orchestra rose to international prominence under Vivaldi's direction. He was promoted to music director in 1716.

Vivaldi's early fame as a composer and musician did not translate into long-term financial __success__. After being overshadowed by younger composers and more modern styles, Vivaldi left Venice for Vienna, Austria, possibly hoping to find a position in the imperial court there. Following the __death__ of Charles VI, he found himself without a prominent patron and died in poverty in Vienna on July 28, 1741. He was laid to rest in a simple grave following a funeral service devoid of music.

In the early twentieth century, musicians and scholars revived Vivaldi's music, and many of the composer's unknown works were recovered from obscurity. In 1939, Alfredo Casella, a composer, and __pianist__ organized the revival of Vivaldi Week. Since World War II, Vivaldi's music has been widely performed. The choral composition Gloria, which was reintroduced to the public during Casella's Vivaldi Week, is particularly well-known and is regularly __performed__ at Christmas celebrations worldwide.

Vivaldi's work, which included nearly 500 concertos, influenced later composers such as Johann __Sebastian__ Bach.

# Science Multiple Choice
# Quiz: Food Chain and Food
# Web

Select the best answer for each question.

1. In ecology, it is the sequence of transfers of matter and energy in the form of food from organism to organism.
   a. Food Chain
   b. Food Transport
   c. Food Sequencing

2. _____ can increase the total food supply by cutting out one step in the food chain.
   a. Birds
   b. People
   c. Animals

3. Plants, which convert solar energy to food by photosynthesis, are the _____.
   a. secondary food source
   b. tertiary food source
   c. primary food source

4. _____ help us understand how changes to ecosystems affect many different species, both directly and indirectly.
   a. Food Chain
   b. Food Web
   c. Food Transport

5. _____ eat decaying matter and are the ones who help put nutrients back into the soil for plants to eat.
   a. Decomposers
   b. Consumers
   c. Producers

6. _____ are producers because they produce energy for the ecosystem.
   a. Plants
   b. Decomposers
   c. Animals

7. Each organism in an ecosystem occupies a specific _____ in the food chain or web.
   a. trophic level
   b. space
   c. place

8. What do you call an organism that eats both plants and animals?
   a. Herbivores
   b. Carnivores
   c. Omnivores

9. Carnivore is from the Latin words that means _____.
   a. "plant eaters"
   b. "eats both plants and animals"
   c. "flesh devourers"

10. A food web is all of the interactions between the species within a community that involve the transfer of energy through _____.
    a. reservation
    b. consumption
    c. adaptation

11. Why are animals considered consumers?
    a. because they don't produce energy, they just use it up
    b. because they produce energy for the ecosystem
    c. because they only produce energy for themselves

12. How do plants turn sunlight energy into chemical energy?
    a. through the process of photosynthesis
    b. through the process of adaptation
    c. through the process of cancelation

# Science Multiple Choice Quiz: Temperate Forest Biome

Select the best answer for each question.

1. _____ are found in Northern Hemisphere regions with moist, warm summers and cold winters, primarily in eastern North America, eastern Asia, and western Europe.

   a. Deciduous forests

   b. Wild forests

   c. Rainforests

2. How many types of forest biomes are there?

   a. 2

   b. 3

   c. 4

3. Temperate forests emerged during the period of global cooling that began at the beginning of the _____.

   a. Medieval Era

   b. Paleozoic Era

   c. Cenozoic Era

4. Major temperate forests are located in the following areas, except for:

   a. Eastern China

   b. Japan

   c. Korea

5. What makes a forest a temperate forest?

   a. Temperature, Two seasons, Tropics, and Clay soil.

   b. Temperature, Climate, Wet season, and Loam soil.

   c. Temperature, Four seasons, Lots of rain, and Fertile soil.

6. The three main types of forest biomes are: the rainforest, the temperate forest, and the _____.

   a. Coniferous

   b. Taiga

   c. Broad-leafed

7. Many trees rely on _____ to get through the winter.

   a. temperature

   b. sap

   c. rain

8. Temperate forests are usually classified into two main groups, and these are: _____ and _____.

   a. Deciduous, Evergreen

   b. Coniferous, Deciduous

   c. Indigenous, Evergreen

9. Deciduous is a Latin word that means _____.

   a. "to rise up"

   b. "to subside"

   c. "to fall off"

10. Certain trees in a temperate forest can grow up to how many feet?

    a. 50 feet tall

    b. 90 feet tall

    c. 100 feet tall

11. _____ forests are made up mostly of conifer trees such as cypress, cedar, redwood, fir, juniper, and pine trees.

    a. Broad-leafed

    b. Mixed coniferous and broad-leafed

    c. Coniferous

12. The animals that live in temperate forests have _____ that allow them to _____ in different kinds of weather.

    a. adaptations, survive

    b. compatibility, survive

    c. conformity, thrive

# Social Skill Interests: Things To Do

A **hobby** is something that a person actively pursues relaxation and enjoyment. On the other hand, a person may have an **interest** in something because they are curious or concerned. Hobbies usually do not provide monetary compensation. However, a person's interests can vary and may lead to earning money or making a living from them. Hobbies are typically pursued in one's spare time or when one is not required to work. Interests can be followed in one's spare time or while working, as in the case of using one's passion as a source of income. A hobby can be a recreational activity that is done regularly in one's spare time. It primarily consists of participating in sports, collecting items and objects, engaging in creative and artistic pursuits, etc. The desire to learn or understand something is referred to as interest. If a person has a strong interest in a subject, he or she may pursue it as a hobby. However, an interest is not always a hobby. Hobbies such as stamp and flower collecting may not be a source of income for a person, but the items collected can sometimes be sold. Hobbies frequently lead to discoveries and inventions. Interests could be a source of income or something done for free. If a person is interested in cooking or enjoys creating dishes, he can do so at home or make it a career by becoming a chef.

_____

*Put the words in the correct category.*

| | | | | | |
|---|---|---|---|---|---|
| pottery | card making | candle making | reading | weaving | knitting |
| gym | jewellery | chess | surfing | computer games | collecting |
| woodwork | Soccer | art | swimming | cooking | skateboarding |
| embroidery | skiing | gardening | writing | chatting | sewing |
| netball | stamp collecting | football | music | rugby | basketball |

| Sport (10) | Handcrafts (10) | Interests (10) |
|---|---|---|
| Soccer | knitting | reading |
| rugby | sewing | cooking |
| football | card making | music |
| netball | woodwork | stamp collecting |
| basketball | weaving | gardening |
| surfing | jewellery | chess |
| skateboarding | pottery | computer games |
| skiing | candle making | writing |
| swimming | embroidery | collecting |
| gym | art | chatting |

# Health: Check Your Symptoms

1. **I've got a pain in my head.**
   a. Stiff neck
   b. headache

2. **I was out in the sun too long.**
   a. Sunburn
   b. Fever

3. **I've got a small itchy lump or bump.**
   a. Rash
   b. Insect bite

4. **I might be having a heart attack.**
   a. Cramps
   b. Chest pain

5. **I've lost my voice.**
   a. Laryngitis
   b. Sore throat

6. **I need to blow my nose a lot.**
   a. Runny nose
   b. Blood Nose

7. **I have an allergy. I have a**
   a. Rash
   b. Insect bite

8. **My shoe rubbed my heel. I have a**
   a. Rash
   b. Blister

9. **The doctor gave me antibiotics. I have a/an**
   a. Infection
   b. Cold

10. **I think I want to vomit. I am**
   a. Nauseous
   b. Bloated

11. **My arm is not broken. It is**
   a. Scratched
   b. Sprained

12. **My arm touched the hot stove. It is**
   a. Burned
   b. Bleeding

13. **I have an upset stomach. I might**
   a. Cough
   b. Vomit

14. **The doctor put plaster on my arm. It is**
   a. Sprained
   b. Broken

15. **If you cut your finger it will**
   a. Burn
   b. Bleed

16. **I hit my hip on a desk. It will**
   a. Burn
   b. Bruise

17. **When you have hay-fever you will**
   a. Sneeze
   b. Wheeze

18. **A sharp knife will**
   a. Scratch
   b. Cut

# Art: Roman Portrait Sculptures

| | | | | |
|---|---|---|---|---|
| Alexander | aristocrats | ancestral | shrine | rewarded |
| sculpture | pattern | mosaics | marble | artistic |

Portrait  sculpture  has been practiced since the beginning of Roman history. It was most likely influenced by the Roman practice of creating  ancestral  images. When a Roman man died, his family made a wax sculpture of his face and kept it in a special  shrine  at home. Because these sculptures were more like records of a person's life than works of art, the emphasis was on realistic detail rather than  artistic  beauty.

As Rome became more prosperous and gained access to Greek sculptors, Roman  aristocrats  known as patricians began creating these portraits from stone rather than wax.

Roman sculpture was about more than just honoring the dead; it was also about honoring the living. Important Romans were  rewarded  for their valor or greatness by having statues of themselves erected and displayed in public. This is one of the earliest of these types of statues that we've discovered, and the  pattern  continued all the way until the Republic's demise.

The mosaic is the only form of Roman art that has yet to be discussed. The Romans adored mosaics and created them with exquisite skill. The Romans created  mosaics  of unprecedented quality and detail using cubes of naturally colored  marble . The floor mosaic depicting  Alexander  the Great at the Battle of Issus is probably the most famous Roman mosaic.

# Parts of Speech Matching

- NOUN. used to identify any of a class of people, places, or things
- PRONOUN. a word (such as I, he, she, you, it, we, or they) that is used instead of a noun or noun phrase
- VERB. a word used to describe an action, state, or occurrence
- ADJECTIVE. modify or describe a noun or a pronoun
- ADVERB. word that modifies (describes) a verb (she sings loudly), adverbs often end in -ly
- PREPOSITION. word or phrase that connects a noun or pronoun to a verb or adjective in a sentence
- CONJUNCTION. word used to join words, phrases, sentences, and clauses
- INTERJECTION. word or phrase that expresses something in a sudden or exclamatory way, especially an emotion

| | | | | |
|---|---|---|---|---|
| 1 | C | Identify the noun. | ⇢ | Lion |
| 2 | I | Identify the verb. | ⇢ | barked |
| 3 | F | What is an adjective? | ⇢ | a word that describes nouns and pronouns |
| 4 | B | Three sets of nouns | ⇢ | mother, truck, banana |
| 5 | E | Three sets of adverbs | ⇢ | always, beautifully, often |
| 6 | G, H | above, across, against | ⇢ | preposition |
| 7 | D | but, and, because, although | ⇢ | conjunctions |
| 8 | J | Wow! Ouch! Hurrah! | ⇢ | Interjection |
| 9 | A | Mary and Joe are friends. | ⇢ | verb |
| 10 | G, H | Jane ran <u>around</u> the corner yesterday. | ⇢ | preposition |

[Student worksheet has a 4 line writing exercise here.]

# Grammar: Contractions
# Multiple Choice

**Simply put, you replace the letter(s) that were removed from the original words with an apostrophe when you make the contraction.**

1. Here is
   a. Here's
   b. Heres'

2. One is
   a. Ones'
   b. One's

3. I will
   a. Il'l
   b. I'll

4. You will
   a. You'll
   b. Yo'ill

5. She will
   a. She'll
   b. She'ill

6. He will
   a. He'ill
   b. He'll

7. It will
   a. It'ill
   b. It'll

8. We will
   a. We'll
   b. We'ill

9. They will
   a. They'ill
   b. They'll

10. That will
    a. That'l
    b. That'll

11. There will
    a. There'ill
    b. There'll

12. This will
    a. This'll
    b. This'ill

13. What will
    a. What'ill
    b. What'll

14. Who will
    a. Who'll
    b. Whol'l

# Grammar:
# Subjunctive Mood

Wishes, proposals, ideas, imagined circumstances, and assertions that are not true are all expressed in the subjunctive mood. The subjunctive is frequently used to indicate an action that a person hopes or wishes to be able to undertake now or in the future. In general, a verb in the subjunctive mood denotes a scenario or state that is a possibility, hope, or want. It expresses a conditional, speculative, or hypothetical sense of a verb.

When verbs of advice or suggestion are used, the subjunctive mood is utilized. After verbs of recommendation or advice, the subjunctive appears in a phrase beginning with the word -that.

Here are a few verbs that are commonly used in the subjunctive mood to recommend or advise.

- advise, ask, demand, prefer

1. Writers use the subjunctive mood to express _____ or _____ conditions.
   a. imaginary or hoped-for
   b.

2. Which is NOT a common marker of the subjunctive mood?
   a.
   b. memories

3. Which is NOT an example of a hope-for verb?
   a. demand
   b. need

4. Subjunctive mood is used to show a situation is not _____.
   a. fictional or fabricated
   b. entirely factual or certain

5. Which of the below statements is written in the subjunctive mood?
   a. I wish I were a millionaire.
   b. What would you do with a million dollars?

6. The indicative mood is used to state facts and opinions, as in:
   a. My mom's fried chicken is my favorite food in the world.
   b. Smells, taste, chew

7. The imperative mood is used to give commands, orders, and instructions, as in:
   a. Eat your salad.
   b. I love salad!

8. The interrogative mood is used to ask a question, as in:
   a. Have you eaten all of your pizza yet?
   b. I ordered 2 slices of pizza.

9. The conditional mood uses the conjunction "if" or "when" to express a condition and its result, as in:
   a. Blue is my favorite color, so I paint with it often.
   b. If I eat too much lasagna, I'll have a stomach ache later.

10. The subjunctive mood is used to express wishes, proposals, suggestions, or imagined situations, as in:
    a. Yesterday was Monday, and I ate pizza.
    b. I prefer that my mom make pasta rather than tuna.

# Biology Vocabulary Words Crossword

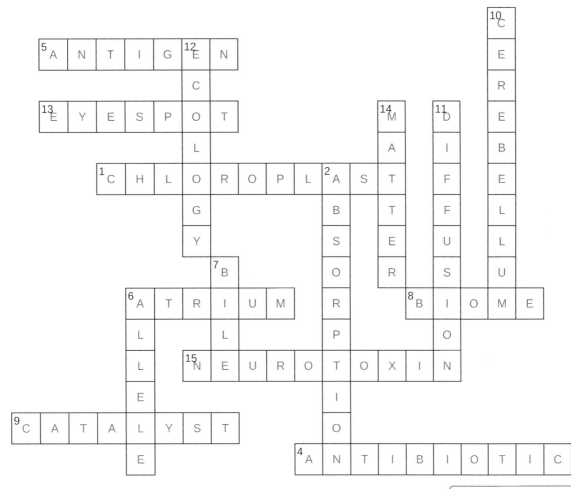

## Across

1. organelle in which photosynthesis takes place
4. a substance used to kill microorganisms and cure infections
5. any substance that stimulates an immune response in the body
6. a chamber connected to other chambers or passageways
8. major ecological community with distinct climate and flora
9. substance that initiates or accelerates a chemical reaction
13. an eyelike marking
15. any toxin that affects neural tissues

## Down

2. a process in which one substance permeates another
6. any of the forms of a gene that can occupy the same locus
7. a digestive juice secreted by the liver
10. a major division of the vertebrate brain
11. the act of dispersing something
12. the environment as it relates to living organisms
14. that which has mass and occupies space

ATRIUM   BIOME   ANTIGEN
ECOLOGY
CHLOROPLAST   MATTER
ABSORPTION   ANTIBIOTIC
DIFFUSION   ALLELE
EYESPOT   NEUROTOXIN
BILE   CEREBELLUM
CATALYST

# Biology: Reading Comprehension Viruses

When we catch a cold or get the flu, we are dealing with the effects of a viral infection. Viruses, despite sharing some characteristics with living organisms, are neither cellular nor alive. The presence of cells, the ability to reproduce, the ability to use energy, and the ability to respond to the environment are all important characteristics of living organisms. A virus cannot perform any of these functions on its own.

A virus, on the other hand, is a collection of genetic material encased in a protective coat, which is typically made of proteins. Viruses are obligate parasites because they must replicate on the host. To replicate itself, a virus must first attach to and penetrate a host cell, after which it will go through the various stages of viral infection. These stages are essentially the virus lifecycle. A virus can enter the host cell via one of several methods by interacting with the surface of the host cell. The virus can then replicate itself by utilizing the host's energy and metabolism.

Bacteriophages, viruses that infect bacteria, either use the lysogenic cycle, in which the host cell's offspring carry the virus, or the lytic cycle, in which the host cell dies immediately after viral replication. Once viral shedding has occurred, the virus can infect additional hosts. Viral infections can be productive in the sense that they cause active infection in the host, or they can be nonproductive in the sense that they remain dormant within the host. These two types of infection can result in chronic infections, in which the host goes through cycles of illness and remission, as well as latent infections, in which the virus remains dormant for a period of time before causing illness in the host.

1. A virus is encased in a protective coat, which is typically made of _____.
   a. proteins
   b. molecules
   c. cells

2. To replicate itself, a virus must first attach to and penetrate a ___ cell.
   a. healthy
   b. living atom
   c. host

3. Viruses are neither cellular nor __.
   a. alive
   b. moving
   c. a threat

4. The virus can replicate itself by utilizing the host's ___and ___.
   a. cells and DNA
   b. molecules and cell
   c. energy and metabolism

5. A virus can remain _____ for a period of time before causing illness in a host.
   a. metabolized
   b. dormant
   c. infected

# History Reading Comprehension: Storming of the Bastille

1. The  French  Revolution began with a violent attack on the government by the people of France.
2. During the Hundred Years' War, the Bastille was a  fortress  built in the late 1300s to protect Paris.
3. By the late 1700s, King Louis XVI had primarily used the Bastille as a state  prison .
4. The majority of the revolutionaries who stormed the Bastille were Paris-based  craftsmen  and store owners.
5. They belonged to the Third Estate, a French social class. Approximately  1000  men carried out the attack.
6. The Third Estate had recently made the king's demands, including a more significant say in government for the  commoners .
7. The Bastille was rumored to be full of political  prisoners  and symbolized the king's  oppression  to many.
8. It also had gunpowder stores, which the revolutionaries required for their  weapons .
9. They demanded that the Bastille's  military  commander, Governor de Launay, hand over the prison and the gunpowder.
10. They began to try to break into the main  fortress  once they were inside the courtyard.
11. **Fearful** soldiers in the Bastille opened fire on the crowd.
12. The  battle  had begun. When some of the soldiers joined the crowd's side, the fight took a turn for the worse.
13. The crowd  assassinated  Governor de Launay and three of his officers after they surrendered.
14. The revolutionaries' success inspired commoners throughout France to rise up and fight against the nobles who had  ruled  them for so long.

# History Reading Comprehension: The Great Depression

During the 1930s, the United States experienced a severe economic downturn known as the Great Depression. It started in the United States, Wall Street to be exact, but quickly spread throughout the rest of the world. Many people were out of work, hungry, and homeless during this period. People in the city would wait for hours at soup kitchens to get a bite to eat. Farmers struggled in the Midwest, where a severe drought turned the soil into dust, resulting in massive dust storms.

America's "Great Depression" began with a dramatic stock market crash on "Black Thursday," October 24, 1929, when panicked investors who had lost faith in the American economy quickly sold 16 million shares of stock. However, historians and economists attribute the Great Depression to a variety of factors, including drought, overproduction of goods, bank failures, stock speculation, and consumer debt.

When the Great Depression began, Herbert Hoover was President of the United States. Many people held Hoover responsible for the Great Depression. The shantytowns where homeless people lived were even dubbed "Hoovervilles" after him. Franklin D. Roosevelt was elected president in 1933. He promised the American people a "New Deal."

The New Deal was a set of laws, programs, and government agencies enacted to aid the country in its recovery from the Great Depression. Regulations were imposed on the stock market, banks, and businesses as a result of these laws. They assisted in putting people to work and attempted to house and feed the poor. Many of these laws, such as the Social Security Act, are still in effect today.

The Great Depression came to an end with the outbreak of World War II. The wartime economy re-employed many people and filled factories to capacity.

The Great Depression left an indelible imprint on the United States. The New Deal laws expanded the government's role in people's daily lives significantly. In addition, public works improved the country's infrastructure by constructing roads, schools, bridges, parks, and airports.

Between 1929 and 1933, the stock market lost nearly 90% of its value.
During the Great Depression, approximately 11,000 banks failed, leaving many people without savings.

1. The Great Depression began with the _____.
   a. World War II
   b. economy drought
   c. stock market crash

2. Who was President when the Great Depression began?
   a. Herbert Hoover
   b. George W Bush
   c. Franklin D. Roosevelt

3. The New Deal was a set of _____.
   a. laws, programs, and government agencies
   b. city and state funding
   c. stock market bailout

4. The Great Depression came to an end with the outbreak of ____.
   a. new laws
   b. investors funding
   c. World War II

# History: King Tut Reading Comprehension

1. **What was King Tut's real name?**
   a. Tutankhaion
   b. Tutankhaten
   c. Tutankhamun

2. **Tut's father died when he was _____ years old.**
   a. 19 yrs old
   b. Twenty-Two
   c. seven

3. **Tutankhamun died when he was about _____ years old.**
   a. nineteen
   b. 16 years old
   c. 21

4. **Nefertiti was the wife of___.**
   a. Tut
   b. Horemheb
   c. Pharaoh Akhenaten

5. **The tomb of young pharaoh Tut is located in the _____.**
   a. Tuts King Egypt
   b. Maine Valley Sons
   c. Valley of the Kings

# Jobs and Careers

Tip: After you've answered the easy ones, go back and work on the harder ones.

| | | | | |
|---|---|---|---|---|
| skill | climbing | monetary | professional | hourly |
| variety | salaried | experience | graduate | achieve |

You might have heard that the education you receive and the information you learn in school will help you get a job when you

__graduate__ . Or your abilities and skills will benefit you in your future careers. So, what's the truth? How do people decide whether they

want a job or a career?

There are several common misconceptions regarding the distinctions between a job and a career. Some people believe that a job is

simply an __hourly__ position, whereas a __salaried__ position is a career. Others believe that a career requires a longer educational path

that results in exceptional skills and knowledge. The truth is not what most people believe.

A job is a position or set of duties performed for __monetary__ gain, whereas a career is a focused path or journey that a person takes to

achieve their professional goals. A career can include a variety of jobs along a career path.

Parents and teachers frequently ask their children what they want to be when they grow up. A career is the answer to that question. A

career is a path or __professional__ journey that a person follows throughout their working life. A career can necessitate extensive

education, such as that of a doctor or a lawyer, or it can require extensive __skill__ training, such as that of an electrician or plumber.

The words "career" and "path" are frequently used interchangeably. A career path is a path that people take to __achieve__ their

professional objectives. Many people work for decades on their career paths, which often include a __variety__ of jobs along the way.

With each job, a person gains __experience__ and skills that will help them get a better job and achieve their career goals.

Another term associated with careers is the concept of people __climbing__ a "career ladder". When people climb the metaphorical

career ladder, they progress step by step from one better job to the next. Careers take years to develop and achieve. Sometimes a lot of

education is required at the start of a career before a person can start moving up the ladder, whereas other careers require years of

experience in the field to get to the top.

# 1 Proofreading Shakespeare: Romeo and Juliet

There are **24** mistakes in this passage. 5 capitals missing. 3 unnecessary capitals. 4 unnecessary apostrophes. 3 punctuation marks missing or incorrect. 2 incorrect homophones. 7 incorrectly spelled words.

In 1597, William Shakespeare published "Romeo and ~~Juliet"~~ **Juliet,"** which would go on to become one of the world's most famous love stories. The plot of Shakespeare's ~~pley~~ **play** takes place in Verona, where the two main ~~characters~~ **characters,** ~~romeo~~ **Romeo** and Juliet, meet and fall in ~~love~~ **love.** Both are descended from two feuding families, the Capulets, and the Montagues. As a result, ~~thay~~ **they** choose to keep their ~~luve~~ **love** hidden and are married by Friar Laurence. Romeo gets into a fight with ~~Juliet"s~~ **Juliet's** cousin Tybalt, whom he ~~Kills~~ **kills** in a ~~Brawl~~ **brawl** despite his best efforts. Romeo is expelled from Verona and escapes to Mantua.

When ~~juliet's~~ **Juliet's** parents press her to marry, she ~~Seeks~~ **seeks** the assistance of Friar Laurence once more, who provides her with a sleeping potion designed to simulate her death. In a letter that never reaches Romeo, he explains his plan. Disgusted by the alleged death of his beloved Juliet, ~~Rumeo~~ **Romeo** returns to Verona and commits suicide at Juliet's open coffin. Juliet awakens from her slumber, sees what has happened, and decides to end her ~~liphe.~~ **life.** The two feuding families now recognize their complicity and reconcile at their children's graves.

The medieval old town of Verona is ideal for putting oneself in the shoes of Romeo and ~~juliet.~~ **Juliet.** Every year, many loving couples and tourists come to walk in the footsteps of ~~romeo~~ **Romeo** and Juliet. A photograph of Juliet's famous balcony, a visit to Romeo's home, or ~~sum~~ **some** ~~queit~~ **quiet** time spent at Julia's grave. No matter ~~were~~ **where** you look in the city, you ~~wall~~ **will** find loving ~~couple's~~ **couples** who stick declarations of love and initials on small slips of paper to the walls or immortalize ~~themselve's~~ **themselves** on the walls or stones of ~~house's~~ **houses** - often illegally.

Although Shakespeare's drama never corresponded to reality, ~~verona~~ **Verona** has a unique charm, especially for lovers, who imagine they can feel the true story behind the literary work, almost as if Romeo and Juliet had really existed.

# Financial: Money, Stocks and Bonds

Three important __conditions__ must be met in order for something to qualify as a financial asset.

As a result, financial assets differ from physical assets such as land or __gold__.

You can touch and feel the actual physical asset with land and gold, but you can only touch and feel something (usually a __piece__ of paper) that represents the asset of value with financial assets.

Money is a government-defined official medium of __exchange__ that consists of cash and __coins__.

Money, __currency__, cash, and legal tender all refer to the same thing.

They are all __symbols__ of a central bank's commitment to keep money's value as stable as possible.

Money is obviously a __valuable__ financial asset. We would all have to __barter__ with one another without a common medium of exchange, trading whatever __goods__ and __services__ we have for something else we need, or trade what we have for something else we could then trade with someone else who has what we need.

Stock is another crucial financial asset in the US __economy__.

Stock, like money, is simply a piece of paper that represents something of value. The something of value' represented by stock is a __stake__ in a company.

Stock is also known as 'equity' because you have a stake in its __profits__ when you own stock in a company.

Jane, her parents, a friend, and her brother are now all __shareholders__ in her company.

The complexities arise when we attempt to assign a __monetary__ value to that stock. A variety of factors determines a stock's __value__.

These are the most basic and fundamental factors that can influence the value of a share of stock. Individual stock __prices__ are affected by macroeconomic trends as well.

Thousands of books have been written in an attempt to discover the __golden__ rule that determines the exact value of a share of stock.

The New York Stock Exchange and __NASDAQ__ were the world's two largest stock exchanges in 2014. (both located in the United States).

When an organization, such as a company, a city or state, or even the federal government, requires funds, bonds can be __issued__. Bonds come in various forms, but they are all debt instruments in which the bondholder is repaid their __principal__ investment, plus interest, at some future maturity date.

The only way a bondholder's money is lost is if the entity that issued the bond declares __bankruptcy__. Bonds are generally safer investments than stocks because they are a legal __obligation__ to repay debt, whereas stocks represent ownership, which can make or lose money.

# How It's Made: Money

1. The _____ agency is in charge of money creation.
   a. federal
   b. government

2. The United States Mint produces coins and dollar bills.
   a. True - coins and dollar bills
   b. False - only coins

3. Each side of a sheet of banknotes must dry for ____ hours.
   a. 72
   b. 24

4. Dollar bills and computer paper don't have the same _____ and feel.
   a. design
   b. weight

5. The metal sheets are fed into a machine that punches out _____.
   a. coins
   b. silver dollars

6. United States Bureau of _____ produces dollar notes.
   a. Engraving and Printing
   b. Engravers and Commission

7. The Secretary of the _____ selects one of the designs submitted by the designers for production.
   a. Treasury
   b. Bank

8. Coins in the United States are created from a combination of _____.
   a. metals and alloys
   b. silver and nickels

9. Before being stamped with the design, the blank coins are _____.
   a. heated and cleaned
   b. shined and reserved

10. Paper money is created from a particular _____ blend, it is more difficult to forge.
   a. parcel and green dye
   b. cotton and linen

# Introvert vs. Extrovert

Introvert is a person who prefers calm environments, limits social engagement, or embraces a greater than average preference for solitude.

**SYNONYMS:**
brooder
loner
solitary

**Extrovert** is an outgoing, gregarious person who thrives in dynamic environments and seeks to maximize social engagement.

**SYNONYMS:**
character
exhibitionist
show-off
showboat

------------------------------

Fill in the blank with the correct word. [ introvert, introverts, extrovert, extroverts]

1. Sue is the __extrovert__ in the family; opinionated, talkative and passionate about politics.

2. He was described as an __introvert__, a reserved man who spoke little.

3. __Extroverts__ are often described as the life of the party.

4. An __introvert__ is often thought of as a quiet, reserved, and thoughtful individual.

5. __Extroverts__ enjoy being around other people and tend to focus on the outside world.

6. Typically __introverts__ tend to enjoy more time to themselves.

7. Jane is an __introvert__ whose only hobby is reading.

8. I am still not as "outgoing" as an __extrovert__ is.

9. I had been a very __extrovert__ person, living life to the full.

10. I am an __introvert__, I am a loner.

11. Because Pat is an __extrovert__ who enjoys chatting with others, she is the ideal talk show host.

12. She is basically an __introvert__, uncomfortable with loud women and confrontations.

# Dealing With Acne

Acne is a skin disorder that results in bumps. Whiteheads, blackheads, pimples, and pus-filled bumps are all sorts of blemishes. What's the source of these annoying bumps? Pores and hair follicles make up most of your skin's top layer. Sebum (pronounced "see-bum"), the natural oil that moisturizes hair and skin, is produced in the pores by oil glands.

Generally, the glands produce adequate sebum, and the pores are good. However, oil, dead skin cells, and bacteria can block a pore if they accumulate in it to an unhealthy level. Acne may result as a result of this.

Puberty-induced hormonal changes are to blame for acne in children. If your parent suffered from acne as a teen, you will likely as well because your pores may produce more sebum when under stress; stress may worsen acne. Acne is usually gone by the time a person reaches their twenties.

**Here are a few tips for preventing breakouts if you suffer from acne:**

- It would help if you washed your face with warm water and a light soap or cleanser in the morning before school and before bed.
- Avoid scrubbing your face. Acne can be exacerbated by irritating the skin, so scrubbing is not recommended.
- Makeup should be washed off at the end of the day if you wear it.
- Ensure to wash your face after a workout if you've been sweating heavily.
- Acne-fighting lotions and creams are readily available over-the-counter. Talk to your parents or doctor about the options available to you.

Make sure you follow the guidelines on any acne medication you use. If you're unsure whether you're allergic to the cream or lotion, use a small amount at first. If you don't notice results the next day, don't give up. Acne medication can take weeks or months to take effect. If you use more than recommended, your skin may become extremely dry and red.

Acne-suffering children can seek treatment from their doctor. Doctors can prescribe stronger medications than what you can get over the counter.

**The following are some other factors to consider:**

- Avoid touching your face if you can.
- Pimples should not be picked, squeezed, or popped.
- Long hair should be kept away from the face, and it should be washed regularly to reduce oil production.

It is possible to get pimples on the hairline by wearing headgear like baseball caps. Stay away from them if you suspect they're contributing to your acne problems.

Despite their best efforts, many children will get acne at some point in their lives. The situation isn't out of the ordinary.

If you suffer from acne, you now have several options for treating it. Remind yourself of this: You are not alone. Take a look around at your buddies and you'll notice that the majority of children and adolescents are dealing with acne, too!

1. Puberty _____ changes are to blame for acne in children.
   - a. harmonic
   - b. [ hormonal ]

2. Pores and hair _____ make up most of your skin's top layer.
   - a. [ follicles ]
   - b. folate

3. Avoid _____ your face.
   - a. using cleanser
   - b. [ scrubbing ]

4. _____ is the oil that moisturizes hair and skin, is produced in the pores by oil glands.
   - a. Acne
   - b. [ Sebum ]

# Smart Ways to Deal With a Bully

One of the most serious issues in our __society__ today is bullying. It's not uncommon for young people to experience a range of __negative__ emotions due to this. Bullies may use physical force (such as punches, kicks, or shoves) or verbal abuse (such as calling someone a name, making fun of them, or scaring them) to harm others.

Some examples of bullying include calling someone names, stealing from them and __mocking__ them, or ostracizing them from a group.

Some bullies want to be the center of attention. As a strategy to be __popular__ or get what they want, they may believe bullying is acceptable. Bullies are usually motivated by a desire to elevate their own status. As a result of picking on someone else, they can feel more power and authority.

Bullies frequently target someone they believe they can __control__. Kids who are easily agitated or have difficulty standing up for themselves are likely targets. Getting a strong reaction from someone can give bullies the illusion that they have the power they desire. There are times when bullies pick on someone who is more intelligent than them or who looks different from them somehow.

Preventing a Bully's Attack
Do not give in to the bully. Avoid the bully as much as possible. Of course, you aren't allowed to disappear or __skip__ class. However, if you can escape the bully by taking a different path, do so.

Bravely stand your __ground__. Scared people aren't usually the most courageous people. Bullies can be stopped by just showing courage in the face of them. Just how do you present yourself as a fearless person? To send a message that says, "Don't mess with me," stand tall. It is much easier to be brave when you are confident in yourself.

Don't Pay Attention to What the Bully Says or Does. If you can, do your best not to listen to the bully's __threats__. Act as though you aren't aware of their presence and immediately go away to a safe place. It's what bullies want: a big reaction to their teasing and being mean. If you don't respond to a bully's actions by pretending you don't notice or care, you may be able to stop them.

Defend your rights. Pretend you're __confident__ and brave. In a loud voice, tell the bully, "No! Stop it!" Then take a step back or even take off running if necessary. No matter what a bully says, say "no" and walk away if it doesn't feel right. If you do what a bully tells you to do, the bully is more likely to keep bullying you; kids who don't stand up for themselves are more likely to be targeted by bullies.

Don't retaliate by being a bully yourself. Don't fight back against someone who's bullying you or your pals by punching, kicking, or shoving them. __Fighting__ back only makes the bully happier, and it's also risky since someone can be injured. You're also going to be in a lot of trouble. It's essential to stick with your friends, keep safe, and seek adult assistance.

Inform a responsible adult of the situation. Telling an adult if you're being bullied is crucial. Find someone you can confide in and tell them what's going on with you. It is up to everyone in the school, from teachers to principals to parents to lunchroom assistants, to stop the bullies. As soon as a teacher discovers the bullying, the bully usually stops because they are worried that their parents will punish them for their behavior. Bullying is terrible, and everyone who is bullied or witnesses bullying should speak up.

# The Human Bones

1. A baby's body has about ____ bones.
   a. 320
   b. 300

2. The ____, which is like a bowl, holds the spine in place.
   a. pelvis
   b. spinal cord

3. A ____ is where two bones meet.
   a. legs
   b. joint

4. At what age is there no more room for growth?
   a. 25
   b. 18

5. Adults have how many bones?
   a. 206
   b. 200

6. The ____ lets you twist and bend.
   a. hip bones
   b. spine

7. Your skull protects your what?
   a. brain
   b. joints

8. Your ribs protect your what?
   a. Heart, spine, and arms
   b. heart, lung, and liver

9. The ____ connects to a large triangular bone on the upper back corner of each side of the ribcage.
   a. shoulder blade
   b. joints blade

10. You have ____ bones in your arm.
    a. two
    b. three

# US Government: Running for Office

When running for public office, candidates must persuade voters that they are the best candidate for the position. Running for office is a term for this type of endeavor. Running for office can be a full-time job in some cases, such as the __presidential__ race. When running for office, there are a lot of things to do.

To run for office, the first step is to ensure that you meet all of the __requirements__. For example, one must be at least 18 years of age and a US citizen in order to apply.

Almost everyone joins a political party to run for public office these days. The primary election, in which they run to represent that party, is frequently the first election they must win. The Democratic Party and the Republican Party are the two most influential __political__ organizations in the United States today.

Without money, it's challenging to run for office. Candidates frequently use billboards, television commercials, and travel to give speeches to promote their campaigns. All of this comes at a price. The people who want to help a candidate win the election provide them with money. As a result, the budget is established. This is critical, as the person with the most significant __financial__ resources may be able to sway the greatest number of voters, ultimately leading to their victory.

A candidate's campaign staff should be assembled as well. These are people who will assist the candidate in their bid for the presidency. They __coordinate__ volunteers, manage funds, plan events, and generally assist the candidate in winning the election. It is the campaign manager's responsibility to lead the campaign team.

Many candidates attempt to stand out from the crowd by creating a memorable campaign slogan. This is a catchy phrase that will stick in voters' minds as they cast their ballots. Calvin Coolidge and Dwight Eisenhower both had __memorable__ campaign slogans, "I Like Ike" for Eisenhower and "Keep Cool with Coolidge" for Coolidge.

At some point, the candidate will begin a public campaign. A lot of "shaking hands and hugging babies" is involved in the process of running for office. There are a lot of speeches they give __outlining__ what they plan to do when they get into the White House. It's their job to explain why they're better than their rivals.

When a candidate runs for office, they usually take a position on several issues relevant to the position for which they are running. A wide range of topics, such as education, clean water, taxation, war, and __healthcare__, are examples.

The debate is yet another aspect of running for office. At a debate, all of the candidates for a particular office sit down together to discuss their positions on a specific issue. Candidates take turns speaking and responding to each other's arguments during the debate. The outcome of a debate between two candidates can mean the difference between __victory__ and defeat.

After months of campaigning, the election is finally upon us. They'll cast their ballots and then get right back to work. Attending rallies or shaking hands with strangers on the street may be part of their campaign __strategy__. All the candidates can do is wait until the polls close. Family, friends, and campaign members usually gather to see how things turn out. If they are successful, they are likely to deliver a victory speech and then go to a party to celebrate.

Becoming Class President

Start working toward your goal of becoming class or high school president as soon as possible if you want to one day hold that position.

If you want to get involved in student __government__ your freshman year, go ahead and join, but don't hold your breath waiting to be elected president. Elections for the freshman class council are frequently a complete disaster. Since freshman elections are held within a month of the start of school, no one has had a chance to get to know one another. The person elected president is usually the one whose name has been mentioned the most by other students. A lot of the time, it's not based on competence or trust.

Building trust and __rapport__ with your classmates is essential from the beginning of the school year. This is the most crucial step in the process of becoming a Class Officer President.

Electing someone they like and trust is a top __priority__ for today's college students. Be a role model for your students. In order to demonstrate your competence, participate in class discussions and get good grades. Avoid being the class clown or the laziest or most absent-minded member of the group.

Become a part of the students' lives. Attend lunch with a variety of people from various backgrounds. Ask them about their __worries__ and their hopes for the school's future.

Make an effort to attend student __council__ meetings even if you aren't currently a member. If you're interested in joining the student council, you may be able to sit in on their meetings, or you may be able to attend an occasional meeting where non-council members can express their concerns and ideas.

# Your Identity and Reputation Online

Your online identity grows every time you use a social network, send a text, or make a post on a website, for example. Your online  persona  may be very different from your real-world persona – the way your friends, parents, and teachers see you.

One of the best things about having an online life is trying on different personas. If you want to change how you act and show up to people, you can. You can also learn more about things that you like. Steps to help you maintain control on the internet can be taken just like in real life.

Here are some things to think about to protect your online identity and reputation:

Nothing is temporary online. The worldwide web is full of opportunities to connect and share with other people. It's also a place with no " take-backs " or "temporary" situations. It's easy for other people to copy, save, and forward your information even if you delete it.

Add a "private" option for your profiles. Anyone can copy or screen-grab things that you don't want the world to see using social  networking  sites. Use caution when using the site's default settings. Each site has its own rules, so read them to ensure you're doing everything you can to keep your information safe.

Keep your passwords safe and change them often. Someone can ruin your  reputation  by pretending to be you online. The best thing to do is pick passwords that no one can guess. The only people who should know about them are your parents or someone else who you can trust. Your best friend, boyfriend, or girlfriend should not know your passwords.

Don't put up pictures or comments that are  inappropriate  or sexually provocative. In the future, things that are funny or cool to you now might not be so cool to someone else, like a teacher or admissions officer. If you don't want your grandmother, coach, or best friend's parents to see it, don't post it. Even on a private page, it could be hacked or copied and sent to someone else.

Don't give in to unwanted advances. There are a lot of inappropriate messages and requests for money that teenagers get when they're on the web. These things can be scary, weird, or even  embarrassing , but they can also be exciting and fun. Do not keep quiet about being bullied online. Tell an adult you trust right away if a stranger or someone you know is bullying you. It's never a good idea to answer. If you respond, you might say something that makes things even worse.

You can go to www.cybertipline.org to report bad behavior or other problems.

Avoid "flaming" by taking a break now and then. Do you want to send an angry text or comment to someone? Relax for a few minutes and realize that the  remarks  will be there even if you have cooled off or change your mind about them.

People may feel free to write hurtful,  derogatory , or abusive remarks on the internet if they can remain anonymous. We can be painful to others if we share things or make angry comments when we aren't facing someone. If they find out, it could change how they see us. If you wouldn't say it, show it, or do it in person, don't do it online.

Make sure you don't break copyright laws. Don't upload, share, or distribute copyrighted photographs, sounds, or files. Be aware of copyright restrictions. Sharing them is great, but doing so illegally runs the risk of legal  repercussions  down the road.

It's time for a self-evaluation. Take a look at your "digital footprint," which people can find out about you. When you search for your screen name or email address, see what comes up. That's one way to get a sense of what other people think of you online.

In the same way that your  real-life  identity is formed, your online identity and reputation are also formed. It's different when you're on the internet because you don't always have the chance to explain how you feel or what you mean. Thinking about what you're going to say and being responsible can help you avoid leaving an online trail that you'll later be sorry about.

# Proofreading Interpersonal Skills: Peer Pressure

Tony is mingling with a large group of what he considers to be the school's cool kids. Suddenly, someone in the group begins mocking Tony's friend Rob, who walks with a limp due to a physical ~~dasability.~~ **disability.**

They begin to imitate ~~rob's~~ **Rob's** limping and ~~Call~~ **call** him 'lame cripple' and other derogatory terms. Although Tony disapproves of their behavior, he does not want to risk being excluded from the group, and thus joins them in mocking Rob.

Peer pressure is the influence exerted on us by ~~member's~~ **members** of our social group. It can manifest in a variety of ways and can lead to us engaging in behaviors we would not normally ~~consider~~ **consider,** such as Tony joining in and mocking his friend Rob.

However, peer pressure is not always detrimental. Positive peer pressure can motivate us to make better ~~chioces,~~ **choices,** such as studying harder, staying in school, or seeking a better job. ~~Whan~~ **When** others influence us to make poor ~~Choices,~~ **choices,** such as smoking, using illicit drugs, or bullying, we succumb to negative peer pressure. We all desire to belong to a group and fit in, so ~~Developing~~ **developing** strategies for resisting peer pressure when necessary can be beneficial.

Tony and his friends are engaging in bullying by ~~moking~~ **mocking** Rob. Bullying is defined as persistent, ~~unwanted.~~ **unwanted,** aggressive behavior directed toward another person. It is ~~moust~~ **most** prevalent in school-aged children but can also ~~aphfect~~ **affect** adults. Bullying can take on a variety of forms, including the following:

~~· Verbil~~
· **Verbal** bullying is when someone is called names, threatened, or taunted verbally.
· Bullying is physical in nature - ~~hitting~~ **hitting,** spitting, tripping, or ~~poshing~~ **pushing** someone.
· Social ~~Bullying~~ **bullying** is intentionally excluding ~~Someone~~ **someone** from ~~activities~~ **activities,** spreading rumors, or embarrassing ~~sumeone.~~ **someone.**
· Cyberbullying is the act of verbally or socially bullying someone via the internet, such as through social media sites.

Peer pressure exerts a significant influence on an individual's decision to engage in bullying ~~behavoir.~~ **behavior.** In Tony's case, even though Rob is a friend and ~~tony~~ **Tony** would never consider mocking his disability, his desire to belong to a group outweighs his willingness to defend his ~~friend~~ **friend.**

Peer pressure is a strong force that is exerted on us by our social group members. Peer pressure is classified into two types: negative peer pressure, which results in poor decision-making, and positive peer pressure, which influences us to make the correct choices. Adolescents are particularly susceptible to peer pressure because of their desire to fit ~~in~~ **in.**

Peer pressure can motivate someone to engage in bullying behaviors such as mocking someone, threatening to harm them, taunting them online, or excluding them from an activity. Each year, bullying ~~affect's~~ **affects** an astounding 3.2 million school-aged children. ~~Severil~~ **Several** strategies for avoiding peer pressure bullying include the following:

- ~~consider~~ **Consider** your actions by surrounding yourself with good company.
- Acquiring the ability to say no to someone you trust.

Speak up - bullying is never acceptable and is taken ~~extramely~~ **extremely** ~~seroiusly~~ **seriously** in schools and the workplace. If someone is attempting to convince you to bully another person, speaking with a trusted adult such as a teacher, coach, counselor, or coworker can frequently help put ~~thing's~~ **things** into perspective and highlight the issue.

# Proofreading Skills:
# Volunteering

There are **10** mistakes in this passage. 3 capitals missing. 4 unnecessary capitals. 3 incorrect homophones.

Your own life can be changed and the lives of others, through volunteer work. ~~to~~ **To** cope with the news that there has been a disaster, you can volunteer to help those in need. Even if you can't contribute financially, you can donate ~~you're~~ **your** time instead.

Volunteering is such an integral part of the American culture that many high schools require their students to participate in community service to graduate.

When you volunteer, you have the freedom to choose what you'd like to do and who or what you think is most deserving of your time. Start with these ideas if you need a little inspiration. We've got just a few examples here.

Encourage the growth and development of young people. Volunteer as a ~~Camp~~ **camp** counselor, a Big Brother or Big Sister, or an after-school sports program. Special Olympics games and events are excellent opportunities to know children with special needs.

Spend the holidays doing good deeds for others. Volunteer at a food bank or distribute toys to children in need on Thanksgiving Day, and you'll be doing your part to help those in need. ~~your~~ **Your** church, temple, mosque, or another place of worship may also require your assistance.

You can visit an animal shelter and play with the ~~Animals.~~ **animals.** Volunteers are critical to the well-being of shelter animals. (You also get a good workout when you walk rescued dogs.)

Become a member of a political campaign. ~~Its~~ **It's** a great way to learn more about the inner workings of politics if ~~your~~ **you're** curious about it. If you are not able ~~To~~ **to** cast a ballot, you can still help elect your preferred candidate.

Help save the planet. Join a river preservation group and lend a hand. Participate in a park cleanup day in your community. Not everyone is cut out for the great outdoors; if you can't see yourself hauling trees up a hill, consider working in the park's office or education center instead.

Take an active role in promoting health-related causes. Many of us know someone afflicted with a medical condition (like cancer, HIV, or diabetes, for example). ~~a~~ **A** charity that helps people with a disease, such as delivering meals, raising money, or providing other assistance, can make you ~~Feel~~ **feel** good about yourself.

Find a way to combine your favorite things if you have more than one. For example, if you're a fan of kids and have a talent for arts and crafts, consider volunteering at a children's hospital.

# ADDITIONAL ASSIGNMENTS PLANNER

○ MONDAY

○ TUESDAY

○ WEDNESDAY

○ THURSDAY

○ FRIDAY

EXTRA CREDIT WEEKEND WORK
○ SATURDAY / SUNDAY

GOALS THIS WEEK

WHAT TO STUDY

# ADDITIONAL ASSIGNMENTS PLANNER

○ MONDAY

○ TUESDAY

○ WEDNESDAY

○ THURSDAY

○ FRIDAY

EXTRA CREDIT WEEKEND WORK
○ SATURDAY / SUNDAY

GOALS THIS WEEK

WHAT TO STUDY

# GRADES TRACKER

| Week | Monday | Tuesday | Wednesday | Thursday | Friday |
|------|--------|---------|-----------|----------|--------|
| 1 | | | | | |
| 2 | | | | | |
| 3 | | | | | |
| 4 | | | | | |
| 5 | | | | | |
| 6 | | | | | |
| 7 | | | | | |
| 8 | | | | | |
| 9 | | | | | |
| 10 | | | | | |
| 11 | | | | | |
| 12 | | | | | |
| 13 | | | | | |
| 14 | | | | | |
| 15 | | | | | |
| 16 | | | | | |
| 17 | | | | | |
| 18 | | | | | |

**Notes**

# GRADES TRACKER

| Week | Monday | Tuesday | Wednesday | Thursday | Friday |
|------|--------|---------|-----------|----------|--------|
| 1 | | | | | |
| 2 | | | | | |
| 3 | | | | | |
| 4 | | | | | |
| 5 | | | | | |
| 6 | | | | | |
| 7 | | | | | |
| 8 | | | | | |
| 9 | | | | | |
| 10 | | | | | |
| 11 | | | | | |
| 12 | | | | | |
| 13 | | | | | |
| 14 | | | | | |
| 15 | | | | | |
| 16 | | | | | |
| 17 | | | | | |
| 18 | | | | | |

## Notes

# End of the Year Evaluation

Name: _____

Grade/Level: _____ Date: _____

Subjects Studied: _____
_____
_____

Cut out book

Goals Accomplished: _____
_____
_____
_____

Most Improved Areas:_____
_____
_____
_____

Areas of Improvement:_____
_____
_____

| Main Curriculum Evaluation | Satisfied | | A= Above Standards | Final Grades |
|---|---|---|---|---|
| _____ | Yes | No | S= Meets Standards | _____ |
| | | | N= Needs Improvement | |
| | | | 98-100 A+ | |
| | | | 93-97 A | |
| _____ | Yes | No | 90-92 A | _____ |
| | | | 88-89 B+ | |
| _____ | Yes | No | 83-87 B | _____ |
| | | | 80-82 B | |
| | | | 78-79 C+ | |
| _____ | Yes | No | 73-77 C | _____ |
| | | | 70-72 C | |
| _____ | Yes | No | 68-69 D+ | _____ |
| | | | 62-67 D | |
| | | | 60-62 D | |
| _____ | Yes | No | 59 & Below F | _____ |

Most Enjoyed:_____
_____

Least Enjoyed:_____
_____

# Academic Transcript

| STUDENT INFORMATION | SCHOOL INFORMATION |
|---|---|
| **Name:** | **School Name:** |
| **Address:** | **Address:** |
| | |
| **Date of Birth:** **Sex:** | **Phone Number:** |
| **Date of Graduation:** | **Email Address:** |
| **Credits Earned:** **GPA:** | *I do hereby affirm that this official academic record is accurate and complete.* |
| | **Administrator's Signature:** |

| COURSE | 1ST SEM | 2ND SEM | FINAL GRADE | CREDIT | COURSE | 1ST SEM | 2ND SEM | FINAL GRADE | CREDIT |
|---|---|---|---|---|---|---|---|---|---|
| **9th GRADE** | | | **YEAR:** | | **10th GRADE** | | | **YEAR:** | |
| | | | | | | | | | |
| | | | | | | | | | |
| | | | | | | | | | |
| | | | | | | | | | |
| | | | | | | | | | |
| | | | | | | | | | |
| | | | | | | | | | |
| | | | | | | | | | |
| | | | | | | | | | |
| **9TH GRADE CREDITS:** | | **9TH GRADE GPA:** | | | **10TH GRADE CREDITS:** | | **10TH GRADE GPA:** | | |
| **11th GRADE:** | | | **YEAR:** | | **12th GRADE:** | | | **YEAR:** | |
| | | | | | | | | | |
| | | | | | | | | | |
| | | | | | | | | | |
| | | | | | | | | | |
| | | | | | | | | | |
| | | | | | | | | | |
| | | | | | | | | | |
| | | | | | | | | | |
| **11TH GRADE CREDITS:** | | **11TH GRADE GPA:** | | | **12TH GRADE CREDITS:** | | **12TH GRADE GPA:** | | |

**Special Awards/ Activities:**

Made in the USA
Columbia, SC
13 December 2024

49201159R00065